THE WAY OF THE CROSS

BIBLICAL RESOURCES FOR A
GLOBAL ANGLICAN FUTURE

A SIX-WEEK STUDY COURSE

Archbishop Dr Justice Akrofi   (Ghana)
Bishop Wallace Benn   (England)
Bishop Dr Michael Fape   (Nigeria)
The Revd Vaughan Roberts   (England)
Canon Dr Vinay Samuel   (India)
Canon David Short   (Canada)
Archbishop Datuk Yong Ping Chung   (Malaysia)

Foreword by Archbishop Peter Akinola   (Nigeria)

The Latimer Trust

This collection is © to The Latimer Trust

Printed in the UK and distributed worldwide by The Latimer Trust under ISBN 978-0-946307-98-2

Printed in North America and distributed in the USA and Canada by Regent College Publishing under ISBN 978-1-57383-435-3

February 2009

Individual contributors retain copyright to their own work.

Cover photograph: Jerusalem alley © mr.lightning – Fotolia.com

Scripture quotations taken from the HOLY BIBLE, NEW INTERNATIONAL VERSION. Copyright © 1973, 1978, 1984 by International Bible Society.

Used by permission of Hodder & Stoughton Publishers, a member of the Hodder Headline Group. All rights reserved. "NIV" is a registered trademark of International Bible Society. UK trademark number 1448790.

The Latimer Trust
PO Box 26685, London N14 4XQ UK
Web: www.latimertrust.org
E-mail: administrator@latimertrust.org
Views expressed in works published by The Latimer Trust are those of the authors and do not necessarily represent the official position of The Latimer Trust

Regent College Publishing
5800 University Boulevard, Vancouver, BC V6T 2E4 Canada
Web: www.regentpublishing.com
E-mail: info@regentpublishing.com
Views expressed in works published by Regent College Publishing are those of the authors and do not necessarily represent the official position of Regent College (www.regent-college.edu)

Library and Archives Canada Cataloguing in Publication
ISBN-13: 978-1-57383-435-3

Contents

Foreword *Archbishop Peter Akinola*..........................5

Introduction *Canon Dr Vinay Samuel*......................6

1. **Genesis 12 – The Promise of God**
   Archbishop Dr Justice Akrofi..........................8

2. **Exodus 24 – The Presence of God**
   Canon David Short..................................20

3. **2 Samuel 7 – The King of God**
   The Revd Vaughan Roberts..........................32

4. **Luke 24 – The Son of God**
   Bishop Dr Michael Fape............................47

5. **Revelation 21 – The Throne of God**
   Archbishop Datuk Yong Ping Chung................59

6. **Jude – The Authority of God**
   Bishop Wallace Benn...............................73

Appendix: *Jerusalem Statement on the Global Anglican Future,* incorporating *The Jerusalem Declaration* 82

Notes

The authors

These Bible studies seek to embrace the scope of the story of our redemption, which is focused on the Way of the Cross. The authors were leaders and speakers at the Global Anglican Future Conference (www.gafcon.org), held in Jerusalem in June 2008, when 1200 Anglican leaders returned to the roots of their faith in the Holy Land.

Bible study questions

We have created Bible studies based on the teachings given at GAFCON in Jerusalem. We encourage all members of a Bible study group to read those teachings ahead of time, but especially we encourage the leaders to do so in spiritual preparation for leading their groups. However, the focus of the studies should be on the Bible passages; the studies do not attempt simply to reiterate the teachings.

We hope that, in your discussion group, the questions printed at the end of each study will help you to dig into what that study has distilled from the passage, and also to engage with what the study says in relation to the biblical passage. We hope, too, that you will relate the themes of the study to Lenten themes, focusing on the suffering, death and resurrection of Christ.

Recordings

Study groups may like to listen to the audio or video recordings of the 30-minute Bible teaching sessions from GAFCON. Studies 2 and 3 can be downloaded in video form from www.anglican-mainstream.net under the section GAFCON Video and audio. Studies 1-3 can be downloaded in audio form from the same site. Studies 1-4 are available on a CD which has all the public presentations at GAFCON and can be ordered from mainstreamanglican@gmail.com or Anglican Mainstream, 21 High Street, Eynsham, OX29 4HE, England for £2 each plus postage. Studies 1 and 2 are on a DVD and Studies 3 and 4 are on a second DVD. These are also available from the same address for £2 each plus postage.

The Way, the Truth and the Life

Issues discussed at the GAFCON gathering and touched upon in these studies were the subject of the book, *The Way, the Truth and the Life: Theological Resources for a Pilgrimage to a Global Anglican Future*, prepared by the GAFCON Theological Resource Team. It is also available from the Latimer Trust. www.latimertrust.org

Foreword

The Most Revd Peter Akinola
Archbishop of Abuja and Primate of all Nigeria
Chairman, GAFCON Primates' Council

In calling orthodox Anglicans to meet in Jerusalem, we were calling them to return to their roots, both doctrinally, in the Scriptures, and historically, in the Holy Land, where God has acted decisively for our redemption through the Lord Jesus Christ.

Central to the GAFCON gathering were the daily expositions of Scripture, which were followed by group discussion and prayer. We shared stories of our own Christian journey, or pilgrimage, and recognized that the way of the cross is at the heart of our discipleship, and also of our engagement with the world.

We now invite a wider circle of churches to join us in these studies, particularly during the season of Lent, as we consider them under the overall title of *The Way of the Cross*.

It is our hope that the GAFCON movement, and the Fellowship of Confessing Anglicans, will be known for, and marked by, that commitment to the priority of Scriptural teaching that is the mark of authentic Christian faith in the Anglican Communion.

The central problem today is the apostasy of those attempting to rewrite the word of God. There is urgent need for repentance, both on the part of those who seem to have made shipwreck of their most holy faith, and on the part of those whose faith has not fired them sufficiently to stand up and be counted for Christ. Those on the Lord's side must be clearly identifiable, while those who err must return to the fold.

We pray and trust that the Lord will meet with all who seek to follow the Way of the Master's Cross through these studies, and that he will empower them for ever more faithful witness and fruitful discipleship.

+ Peter Akinola

Advent 2008

Introduction
Canon Dr Vinay Samuel

For the message of the cross is foolishness to those who are perishing, but to us who are being saved it is the power of God. (1 Corinthians 1:18)

May I never boast except in the cross of our Lord Jesus Christ, through which the world has been crucified to me, and I to the world. (Galatians 6:14)

For St Paul the cross stands between the Christian and the world. The unbelieving world considers the message signified by the cross as a piece of folly, incapable of bringing the light of truth or of delivering spiritual power. For the believer, however, the message of the cross delivers both truth and power. The believer hears and receives the message of the cross, and also walks in the way of the cross day by day, as Christ's disciple in the world.

The unbelieving world sees the cross as a descent into defeat, not an ascent to divine knowledge, which it is for the believer. The cross *is* a descent in one sense: the believer sees it as the descent to earth of God's power, to lift a fallen world from its captivity to death. The cross also represents the ascent of God's love, restoring his creation to its original purpose. The Way of the Cross is, in the first place, a relationship with the person of Christ and, through that relationship, a pathway to knowledge and action in the world.

The way to the sacred

The Way of the Cross is the way to the sacred, to the divine presence in our world. Hebrews 9:12 says that Christ the High Priest 'entered the Most Holy Place once for all by his own blood'. In Hebrews 9:24 it is written that Christ 'entered heaven itself, now to appear for us in God's presence.' In the Old Testament the human high priest experienced the presence of God directly only once a year. But Christ, the mediator of the new covenant, leads his people into a permanent experience of God's presence, in his incarnated, crucified and risen person. The sacred is not out of reach, to be glimpsed only rarely. In the Way of the Cross the sacred is always with us, his people, and we are in it until the end of time. As we come together in the celebration of the Lord's Supper, we, the community of Christ's disciples, celebrate this entry into the sacred, and our experience of the divine presence in our daily life.

The way to understanding the world

The Way of the Cross is the way to the life and love that constitute us as persons made in God's image. The effect of the fall was to disconnect human personhood from its source in the divine life and love that are at the heart of the personhood of the triune God. Death and violence now dominate human life, but the Way of the Cross reconnects us to the love that is intrinsic to the Trinity, and also to the life that flows from the Son through the Spirit into God's creation. In the Way of the Cross the believer's conscience is cleansed 'from acts that lead to death' (Hebrews 9:14), and is shaped according to the life and love of God himself.

The Way of the Cross opens the disciple to understanding the world as God views it. The disciple sees the world through the cross. The disciple faces the beguilement of the world, for which the evil one, who sees himself as the lord of this world, is responsible. But the cruciform perspective of the Way of the Cross exposes the true nature of the evil one's propaganda, and enables the disciple to address the real world. In this perspective human suffering is seen as not just a curse; rightly endured it can be redemptive and transforming. And the future is seen, not as a blank in which the powerful may fulfil their desires and dreams, but as a God-designed purpose, towards which the whole of history is moving.

The way of the Holy Spirit

The Way of the Cross is the way of the Holy Spirit, who enables the disciple to offer his or her life to God as a living sacrifice. On the cross Christ offered himself to God through the eternal Spirit (Hebrews 9:14), and now the Holy Spirit leads the disciple in the Way of the Cross, empowering him or her to release God's life and love into the world.

The GAFCON bible studies explore the grand biblical story of God's engagement with the world. As you study them in the Lenten season, it is our prayer that they will enrich your relationship with Christ, and lead you deeper in the Way of the Cross.

Canon Dr Vinay Samuel is convenor of the GAFCON Theological Resource Group.

__Canon Dr Vinay Samuel__ and his wife Colleen have led the Divya Shanthi Community Association and Ministries, among disadvantaged communities in Bangalore, India, for over twenty-five years. From this experience, Vinay has developed a Bible-based ministry to Christian leaders, concerning enterprise solutions to poverty and also the role of religion in public life, which operates in all five continents. He was the founder and first director of the Oxford Centre for Mission Studies. He has been a member of the GAFCON leadership team and is the Convenor of the GAFCON Theological Resource Group. He and Colleen have four children and five grandchildren.

STUDY 1: THE PROMISE OF GOD

GENESIS 12

THE CALL OF ABRAM

¹ The LORD had said to Abram, "Leave your country, your people and your father's household and go to the land I will show you.
² I will make you into a great nation and I will bless you;
I will make your name great, and you will be a blessing.
³ I will bless those who bless you, and whoever curses you I will curse; and all peoples on earth will be blessed through you."

⁴ So Abram left, as the LORD had told him; and Lot went with him. Abram was seventy-five years old when he set out from Haran. ⁵ He took his wife Sarai, his nephew Lot, all the possessions they had accumulated and the people they had acquired in Haran, and they set out for the land of Canaan, and they arrived there.

⁶ Abram travelled through the land as far as the site of the great tree of Moreh at Shechem. At that time the Canaanites were in the land. ⁷ The LORD appeared to Abram and said, "To your offspring [a] I will give this land." So he built an altar there to the LORD, who had appeared to him.
⁸ From there he went on toward the hills east of Bethel and pitched his tent, with Bethel on the west and Ai on the east. There he built an altar to the LORD and called on the name of the LORD. ⁹ Then Abram set out and continued toward the Negev.

Genesis 12
The Promise of God

Archbishop Dr Justice Akrofi

What a humbling and frightening privilege, to be invited to lead a biblical exposition at a meeting of the Global Anglican Future conference! Frightening because of daring to speak the word of God, with all my imperfections. Frightening because of the collection of charismata at this conference. Frightening because of the challenge of the context in which we meet. Humbling because of being chosen for the task, when several of us here could have been chosen. Humbling because I am caught between speaking as an individual, and speaking as the representative of the flock and the province entrusted to me in my region. Humbling because of the danger of the exposition becoming a politicisation of the word of God. Be that as it may, as an Anglican who is characteristically rooted in Scripture and tradition, especially in the early Church Fathers – these also inform my humble effort here – I come with a sense of humility, under the mighty hand of God and the weight of our tradition.

Allow me to make one more preliminary comment. The well-known biblical expositor and economist, Hans-Ruedi Weber, once wrote a book with the eloquent title, *The Book That Reads Me*. It was a description of the Bible. The Bible, so to speak, is holding up the word of God like a mirror, to help us see ourselves and be challenged, for the renewal of our lives. There is a dynamic here: on the one hand Scripture is putting questions to the reader, and offering challenges, while on the other the reader is coming to God, in Scripture, and bringing *his* questions. To use the language of the hymn writer, 'Bringing all my burdens, sorrows, sin and care; at thy feet I lay them, and I leave them there'.

My invitation asked me to give a biblical exposition during a plenary session. The particular assignment is Genesis chapter 12. Further, it is designed to be part of a series, which is intended to give a sense of the theological story of the whole Bible. In other words, we are encouraged to avoid a Thomistic view of Genesis 12; the chapter is to be read in the light of the entire Scripture. On this my own Vicar-General has written: 'The story of the entire Bible, from the story of Cain and Abel to the revelation of a new heaven in the book of Revelation, is about the righteousness of God and the indignation of God against the injustice of man. In the final

> **ABRAM IN EGYPT**
>
> [10] Now there was a famine in the land, and Abram went down to Egypt to live there for a while because the famine was severe. [11] As he was about to enter Egypt, he said to his wife Sarai, "I know what a beautiful woman you are. [12] When the Egyptians see you, they will say, 'This is his wife.' Then they will kill me but will let you live. [13] Say you are my sister, so that I will be treated well for your sake and my life will be spared because of you."
>
> [14] When Abram came to Egypt, the Egyptians saw that she was a very beautiful woman. [15] And when Pharaoh's officials saw her, they praised her to Pharaoh, and she was taken into his palace. [16] He treated Abram well for her sake, and Abram acquired sheep and cattle, male and female donkeys, menservants and maidservants, and camels.
>
> [17] But the LORD inflicted serious diseases on Pharaoh and his household because of Abram's wife Sarai. [18] So Pharaoh summoned Abram. "What have you done to me?" he said. "Why didn't you tell me she was your wife? [19] Why did you say, 'She is my sister', so that I took her to be my wife? Now then, here is your wife. Take her and go!" [20] Then Pharaoh gave orders about Abram to his men, and they sent him on his way, with his wife and everything he had.
>
> **Footnotes:**
> a. Genesis 12:7 Or *seed*

Study 1: The Promise of God

analysis, empirically, sociologically and theologically, Satan and the forces of evil are not, and do not have, the last word.' Scripture has affirmed the victory of truth, peace and righteousness, in the final analysis, and I dare to look beyond the present crisis, to the day when God's truth will shine clear and unalloyed. To return to my brief, how does the call of Abraham, set in this drama, build into the final revelation of God's justice and righteousness?

Additionally, I have been asked to undertake this study of Genesis 12 against the background of creation (Genesis 1) and the fall (Genesis 3) – in other words, what light may the biblical stories of God as Creator, and the fall, throw on the further story of the call of Abraham and the covenant with him? The creation is the first affirmation of biblical faith and is therefore fundamental to our biblical faith. The fall describes the fundamental human story and experience of human disobedience and waywardness, towards no lesser a being than the Creator – the hand that feeds humans. What do these various snapshots and insights contribute to the meaning of the call of Abraham, and the covenant between God and the Patriarch Abraham?

The British philosopher, Bertrand Russell, once said, 'The world is a fortuitous collocation of atoms.' In other words, creation happened by chance, and no master plan or master design is needed. By contrast, the Biblical faith is built on the faith that, in the beginning, God, and in the end, God. The Creator God holds the created order in the palm of his hand, creating, redeeming, sustaining and enabling his world. As the basic conviction plays out, two basic affirmations are involved. First, God has been uniquely involved in the origin of earth and sky, and of earth and heaven. Second, as God's creation, the created order is a medium revealing something of God, and is subject to God's will (Romans 1: 13-20). Disobedience to the will of God the Creator incurs the wrath of the Creator; there is an irreconcilable opposition between good and evil.

That is the backdrop to the crisis over sexuality. Yes, the Creator God is loving, and he has promised to save. But

Study 1: The Promise of God

disobedience carries with it its own consequences, in terms of God's wrath. God's claim on people and on their destiny is immoveable.

There is a further note that should not be overlooked. Humanity, male and female, is the culmination of God's creation. The key phrase in the understanding of this culmination comes from God, 'Let us make man in our image, in our likeness' (Genesis 1: 26). Humans differ from other created beings, such as animals; we are different because we are created in the image of God, and we bear his image. This fundamental affirmation means, on the one hand, that man may not be reduced to the level of animals. On the other hand, man may not be divinised. The question that must be asked in this crisis is, 'How does our stance foster or detract from the fact that human beings – created to be rational, loving and sociable – are accountable to the transcendent Creator?' So a prime issue in this crisis is, 'What is it like to be truly human in God's image, in God's likeness?'

Fortunately, I am limited to the story of the fall of Adam and Eve, which identifies disobedience to God's will as the cause of disruption between God and man, and between man and man. The African Bible commentary has a crisp summary:

'It is not one's intelligence and charm that are important, but what one does with them. The serpent used its abilities to turn the woman – and through her the man – away from God. The pattern has continued down the centuries, as we see the wicked use all sorts of tricks to mislead the unsuspecting – evil men trick innocent young girls into immoral acts, and unscrupulous people buy valuable items from the needy or ignorant people for a fraction of their value.'

Satan approaches humanity in disguise (2 Corinthians 11:14). And so we might suggest that it is a biblical virtue not to trust appearances. 1 Samuel 16 has these words, 'Do not consider his appearance or his height, for I have rejected him. The Lord does not look at the things man looks at. Man looks at the outward

Let us endeavour to take on board all the various facets of the texts we shall be studying, and see how they relate to the core message of Scripture, which is the incarnation.

Study 1: The Promise of God

appearance, but the Lord looks at the heart.' There are several seductive ideologies around us. May we be encouraged to look beyond the ideologies, and discern the will of God.

Genesis 12 is a chapter of 20 verses. Mercifully, the organising team have given me a code word – 'the Promise of God' – which I am taking as the hermeneutic for reading the entire chapter because, as I mentioned, we must read with a sense of the overarching theological story of the whole Bible. This section, therefore, is to be considered alongside the other themes that will be presented to us – the Presence of God, the King of God, the Son of God and the Throne of God. There is a lesson here: a narrow view of the text may not be adequate for the task before us this week. Let us endeavour to take on board all the various facets of the texts we shall be studying, and see how they relate to the core message of Scripture, which is the incarnation. Indeed, as the letter inviting me put it, 'our conviction is that the present crisis in the Communion has been caused to some extent by the inability of Christians to read each passage in the Bible in the light of the whole.' The promise of God must be heard in balance with the presence of God. The promise of God is that, in the final analysis, God's will will triumph. In the meantime, obedience to the will of God and the worship of God are the only viable options.

Though the code word is 'the promise', the text itself concerns the covenant made between God and Abraham. This covenant marks one of the structural moments in the history of the Hebrews. It marks a relationship of communion between partners, a state of harmonious equilibrium, an important relationship. The relationship is established by this covenant, or compact.

Genesis 12 falls into two sections: first, Abraham, the man of faith, vv1-9, and second, Abraham and Sarah in Egypt, vv10-20.

1. Abraham, the man of faith (vv1-9)

Let me for a moment draw your attention to how God dealt with Abraham. God did not plead with

> *It is interesting to see how the reward for obedience to the will of God is defined. It is defined in terms of 'I will ... I will ...', promises of action to come.*

Abraham. He did not threaten him, either. And Abraham was not left guessing. The lesson here for us, therefore, is that the person who truly listens to God will receive communication from God. People of faith do well to listen to God with obedient hearts, to commune with him. Faith, or trust, in God, and our commitment to God and his will alone, should be our equipment for the struggle.

It is interesting to see how the reward for obedience to the will of God is defined. It is defined in terms of 'I will ..., I will ...', promises of action to come. These predictions call for trust on Abraham's part, a holding on to the fact that what is promised will indeed come to pass. There are four 'I will ...' promises.

1. *'I will make you into a great nation' (v2a).* The curious thing is that the signs were not promising: at that stage Abraham did not even have a child. How could Abraham become the great ancestor when, as yet, he had no children and was advanced in years, and his wife was beyond the age of childbearing? In God's mysterious way Abraham has become a father in faith for a large part of humanity – Jews, Christians and Muslims, the groups of the Abrahamic faith. Let us not be afraid to be the faithful remnant. Let us not be afraid that the whole world may seem to be going after people who do not agree with us. As with Abraham, *the condition for success, for becoming 'ancestors' of great faith and becoming a great nation, is that we should hear and obey the still small voice of God in Scripture, the voice that continues to speak to us.* This is the route to faith, and to our Christian identity.

2. *'I will bless you' (v2b).* God promised he would bless Abraham with many descendents. As recorded in Genesis 15:5, 'He took him outside and said, "Look up at the heavens and count the stars – if indeed you can count them." Then he said to him, "So shall your offspring be."' Also, in Genesis 17:8, God promised Abraham that he would possess the land of Canaan: '"The whole land

STUDY 1: THE PROMISE OF GOD

of Canaan, where you are now an alien, I will give as an everlasting possession to you and your descendents after you, and I will be their God.'" If we are faithful, the promise is that we shall become the vibrant heartland of the gospel of light, to lighten the gentiles. The rapid growth in the churches, in Africa, in Asia, in India, in Canada, in Common Cause congregations in the USA and elsewhere, testify to the fact that faithfulness and obedience to the word of God are the essential ingredients that will make us, as individuals and as congregations, into that vibrant heartland of the gospel of light, bringing people to the saving knowledge of our Lord and Saviour Jesus Christ. In the final analysis, God's cause *will* prevail.

3. *'I will make your name great' (v2c).* This can be a seductive motivation, the desire to have a great name. But, let me say, the fundamental promise is that if we are faithful and obedient to God we, in God's design, may be a power to be reckoned with. It is enough to concentrate on obeying the will of God, without orchestrating the making of a name for ourselves. What is our motivation for the stance we are taking in this crisis? Is it faithfulness to God's word alone, or do we want to make a name for ourselves? Human motives are always mixed; let our motives be pure.

4. *'I will bless those who bless you' (v3a).* The opportunity for obedience to the will of God, and the solidarity we are forging under the canopy of obedience to the will of God, make us not only friends with each other but also, more importantly, friends with God. We are not a clique, nor a faction, nor a political grouping. Through obedience to the will of God we are forging a relationship of friends of God, crossing our provincial and national borders and boundaries. The whole new community is built upon obedient faith in God. Conversely, 'whoever curses you I will curse', God says to Abraham (v3b). All the time that we remain faithful to God, people will call us names but, by the same token, those who oppose us will have to face God's wrath. Decadence may be an example of God's curse on disobedience. In the end, brothers

In the end, brothers and sisters, God is the one in charge, the one who acts. God makes all the promises and he will keep all the promises, so our faith is in him.

and sisters, God is the one in charge, the one who acts. God makes all the promises and he will keep all the promises, so our faith is in him. 'For no matter how many promises God has made, they are "Yes" in Christ. And so through him the "Amen" is spoken by us to the glory of God.' (2 Corinthians 1:20)

2. Abraham and Sarah in Egypt (vv10-20)

The dross alongside the good; darkness alongside light: after all the wonderful things said to Abraham, there is a negative note. In v5b it is reported that Abraham took with him 'the people they had acquired in Haran' – slavery, an evil practice. Abraham, the exemplary paradigm of faith, also followed an evil practice. Religious persons need to be reminded of their tendency towards evil. The Reformers were correct in their diagnosis of the Christian human condition, describing it as *'simul justus et peccator'*; we are at the same time both justified and sinful. This should make us humble, avoiding claims and pretensions to piety and holiness. As we live our Christian lives there is no room for self-righteousness, or supercilious conceit. In my ministry I always have to be on my guard, and see myself as one beggar begging on behalf of other beggars.

Promise is like travelling on the open sea: the further you move away from the coast the more you see the expanse of the sea.

How does this shape my engagement with those with whom I passionately disagree? I will need to reflect on, and take on board, the exhortation of Paul, writing in 2 Corinthians 13:11, 'Aim for perfection, listen to my appeal, be of one mind, live in peace.' Also, the first letter of Peter reminds us that judgment will begin with us, the family of God (1 Peter 4:17). We who may not be guilty of unrighteousness in relation to sexuality will, nevertheless, stand before the judgment seat of God.

There is another example, in this passage, of a contradiction in a life of faith: the deception played by Abraham, the obedient servant of God. In Egypt Abraham contrived a plan to save his own skin. Of course, Sarah's beauty made her attractive to many men. As sure as night follows day, Pharaoh fell for the lie that Sarah was Abraham's sister. Let us learn to tell the truth, and rely on God for his protection. Let us no

Study 1: The Promise of God

> ## Discussion Questions
>
> *Introductory questions: Can you describe very briefly a primary way in which God called you to follow him? What was one of the first things the Lord prompted you to change in your life?*
>
> 1. *God makes wonderful promises to his people. What does this passage teach us about the power of God's words and the place of God's promises in the life of faith?*
>
> 2. *God's blessing on his worldwide church is not always obvious. Are God's promises an unattainable ideal? How may we experience them?*

longer spend precious time and other resources in politicising the painful issue of sexuality in the household of God, to score points. Let us get on with our God-given mission to a dying world, the holistic mission of the church to both young and old, for the empowerment of our women, and for ministering to the many HIV/AIDS patients all around us. In short, let us rescue the perishing, and care for the dying.

3. Three last points

1. No threat, no violence. Throughout the narrative there is a striking absence of threats, vituperation or violence. God communicates his will without threats. God expects voluntary compliance with his will. One is reminded of the saying of Jesus, 'A new command I give you: Love one another.' (John 13:34) May we, out of our own free will and in appreciation of what God has done for us in Christ, yield to the will of God. May we, in this crisis, avoid threats and violence, in any form. Moral decadence is no excuse for violence, be it verbal or physical, nor the bullying of those with whom we disagree.

2. No automatic promise. Allow me to take you to Genesis 12:6a. It was only after Abraham had travelled to the site of the great tree of Moreh at Shechem, that God told

Abraham about the promised land. It is when *we* have set out on a life of obedience to God's will that we shall be initiated into the fullness of God's promise to us. Promise is like travelling on the open sea: the further you move away from the coast the more you see the expanse of the sea. We may not know the details of what our obedience to God's will will mean, in daily life, but as long as we believe that the end waits for the Lord, let us dare to move on, without imagining what the end will be. To use another phrase of my Vicar-General, 'Let us resist the temptation to play at being God's secretaries!'

3. Establishing a tent. After God has promised to give the land of Canaan to his children, Abraham establishes his tent and builds an altar to the Lord (v8). God's promise is a promise of future growth, and Abraham, believing this promise, knows that his descendants will need space in the land in order to build their future. So he takes a first step towards establishing that space, pitching a tent and building an altar. The tent makes the first claim on part of the land, and the altar shows that the whole earth belongs to God, and to no other being. These actions show that worship and spirituality are

3. *'Faith, or trust, in God, and our commitment to his will alone, should be our equipment for the struggle.'* How does Abraham exhibit that in Genesis 12? How does he fail to exhibit that? What are the implications for our own walk with God?

4. What are the key themes concerning the promises of God that are highlighted in this teaching?

5. What is the reality of the promise that the New Covenant offers us, in the light of its fulfilment of the Old Covenant?

6. How do these promises shape and resource our life in the world, and also our engagement with it?

necessary for a life of faith to grow. Growth needs space. This forum in Jerusalem is a kind of space in which to forge a solidarity of obedience and commitment, to faith in God and to his word, the sword of the Spirit. In this space we can affirm one another in being what is right by God, who has graciously entered into a covenant relationship with us.

4. Weaving the threads together

First, the crisis regarding sexuality in the Anglican Communion should neither cloud nor derail our faithful commitment to God our Creator, in whom 'we live and move and have our being.' (Acts 17:28) Paul's starting point for sharing the good news of Jesus Christ with the Athenians is interesting, because the text I have just cited is itself a quotation from the Cretan poet, Epimenides (c.600 BC). Paul is drawing on the glimmers of truth about God that are already present in the Athenian culture. Even if I accept that the gospel critiques my cultural values, I believe my culture still has a thing or two to teach me on the subject of sexuality. My culture frowns upon, and disapproves of, same sex orientation. To go against cultural norms of decency is a very serious derailment of the order of Creation, and of the covenant between God and the children of Abraham.

Secondly, the way forward is to forge solidarity among the faithful remnant, around the globe and the Communion, for the purpose of standing up to be counted on the side of the Creator God, who has sealed the relationship in this sacred covenant.

Thirdly, the covenant goes with a promise. The issue is as yet unresolved, but we dare to hold God to his promise, and plod on with renewed spirituality, forging solidarity and obedience to the will of God. We do so in the conviction that, in the final analysis, God's promise will be fulfilled and God's will will be done. God, in his sovereignty, will rule in justice and righteousness.

Fourthly and finally, it is easy for solidarity to become a way of talking, rather than living. So I commend to us a word of Scripture which we use at the eucharistic celebration, in which Paul urges the Ephesians, and us, 'to live a life worthy of the calling [we] have received. Be completely humble and gentle; be patient, bearing with one another in love. Make every effort to keep the unity of the Spirit through the bond of peace.' (Ephesians 4:1-3)

So now, unto the King

immortal, invisible, the only wise God, ascribe all power, dominion and majesty, now and for evermore. Amen

Archbishop Justice Akrofi is Bishop of Accra, Ghana, and has been Primate of West Africa since 2003. He is married to Maria, a doctor, and they have two children.

Archbishop Akrofi studied in Ghana and in the United States, at Central Connecticut State College (now a university), where he received his B.Sc. and M.Ed. degrees, and also at Yale, where he graduated in 1976 with a Master of Divinity degree. He taught at Cape Coast University and the University of Ghana before serving as Dean of Holy Trinity Cathedral in Accra, and later, from 1996, as Bishop of Accra. In 2000 he received an honorary doctorate from Central Connecticut State University.

In his ministry he has been deeply involved in wholistic mission among poor communities, and has been a director of World Vision Ghana for over twenty years.

Study 1: The Promise of God

Editorial footnote

As we reflect on God's promise to Abram, we can note the following:

- the promise of descendants was given to a couple who were past the age of childbearing
- Abram and Sarai's impatience led to the birth of Ishmael
- Abram had to wait twenty-five years, after the promise, for its fulfilment in Isaac
- Abraham's false satisfaction in Ishmael led to his suggestion to God that Ishmael should be the vehicle of the fulfilment (Genesis 17:18-21), but God answered and reassured him that Isaac would be the covenant child.

During God's twenty-five-year silence Abraham made two attempts to help God:

- with a surrogate Sarah
- with a surrogate child of promise.

God was building Abraham's faith and testing his commitment to the covenant, because the Messiah was destined to come from Isaac's line. God wanted it to be clear that only he could have produced the child of promise at the time he did, so that no one else might share his glory (Isaiah 40).

STUDY 2: THE PRESENCE OF GOD

Exodus 24

THE COVENANT CONFIRMED

¹ Then he said to Moses, "Come up to the LORD, you and Aaron, Nadab and Abihu, and seventy of the elders of Israel. You are to worship at a distance, ² but Moses alone is to approach the LORD; the others must not come near. And the people may not come up with him."
³ When Moses went and told the people all the LORD's words and laws, they responded with one voice, "Everything the LORD has said we will do." ⁴ Moses then wrote down everything the LORD had said.

He got up early the next morning and built an altar at the foot of the mountain and set up twelve stone pillars representing the twelve tribes of Israel. ⁵ Then he sent young Israelite men, and they offered burnt offerings and sacrificed young bulls as fellowship offerings [a] to the LORD. ⁶ Moses took half of the blood and put it in bowls, and the other half he sprinkled on the altar. ⁷ Then he took the Book of the Covenant and read it to the people. They responded, "We will do everything the LORD has said; we will obey."

⁸ Moses then took the blood, sprinkled it on the people and said, "This is the blood of the covenant that the LORD has made with you in accordance with all these words."
⁹ Moses and Aaron, Nadab and Abihu, and the seventy elders of Israel went up ¹⁰ and saw the God of Israel. Under his feet was something like a pavement

Exodus 24
The Presence of God

Canon David Short

I was born in Tanzania, Africa. My father was born in Africa, in Kenya. I was ordained in Sydney, Australia. I work in the diocese of New Westminster and my Archbishop is the Archbishop of the Southern Cone. One of the great joys of being together here is to begin to understand our context. You cannot know me unless you know my context. I cannot know you unless I know your context. And we cannot understand the book of Exodus unless we understand its context. It comes immediately after Genesis, and in the early chapters of Exodus, Moses tells us that God is fulfilling his promises to Abraham (Genesis 12:1-3). The children of God are now a mighty nation. They have been fruitful and they have been multiplying. Now, however, they have become a danger to the Egyptians *because* the blessing of God is resting upon them. But, instead of being in God's place of blessing, they are enslaved in a crushing and brutal bondage. The message of the whole book of Exodus is very important because it is the book of redemption, the book of deliverance. From now on, through the whole of the Scriptures, the way that God will bring his blessing to us and bring us into blessing is through redemption and deliverance. The way that God will fulfil his promises to Abraham and his purposes in creation will be through redemption. The way God brings glory to his name is through redemption.

The book of Exodus teaches us the answers to three questions:
1. What is redemption?
2. Why does God redeem us?
3. How does God redeem us?

1. What is redemption?

The book of Exodus gives us three answers. First, we begin with God's people in slavery, and finish with God's people on the mountain as the glory of God comes down on the tabernacle, and God's people worship and serve him, and rejoice in him. That is what redemption is. It begins with slavery. It is a great freedom from slavery to worship God and to see the glory of God. Redemption is not freedom to do whatever I want. This is the great tragedy of the new gospel in the Anglican churches in the West, certainly in Canada. The new gospel says salvation is God

> *made of sapphire, [b] clear as the sky itself. [11] But God did not raise his hand against these leaders of the Israelites; they saw God, and they ate and drank. [12] The LORD said to Moses, "Come up to me on the mountain and stay here, and I will give you the tablets of stone, with the law and commands I have written for their instruction." [13] Then Moses set out with Joshua his aide, and Moses went up on the mountain of God. [14] He said to the elders, "Wait here for us until we come back to you. Aaron and Hur are with you, and anyone involved in a dispute can go to them."*
>
> *[15] When Moses went up on the mountain, the cloud covered it, [16] and the glory of the LORD settled on Mount Sinai. For six days the cloud covered the mountain, and on the seventh day the LORD called to Moses from within the cloud. [17] To the Israelites the glory of the LORD looked like a consuming fire on top of the mountain. [18] Then Moses entered the cloud as he went on up the mountain. And he stayed on the mountain forty days and forty nights.*
>
> *Footnotes:*
> a. Exodus 24:5 Traditionally *peace offerings*
> b. Exodus 24:10 Or *lapis lazuli*

Study 2: The Presence of God

freeing me to do as I want: that God just accepts me and affirms me just as I am: that I do not need to be changed. But the biblical gospel says that we are redeemed, we are transformed, we are called to be a holy people redeemed by the power of the blood of Jesus Christ, for a life of holiness in the power of the Spirit. When Moses goes to Pharaoh he does not say 'Let my people go to do what they want.' He says, 'Let my people go, so that they may worship me.' (Exodus 8:1,20) True freedom is not freedom to do as I want. It is freedom to serve God in holiness and joy. It is freedom from all that enslaves. It is seeing the vision of the glory of God and living in his presence – that is what redemption is.

It doesn't just happen automatically. You don't just go to sleep one night and wake up in the morning knowing you are free. Exodus teaches us that God has to fight for us. He must defeat all the powers that enslave us and free us from their captivity, because the forces of darkness do not want to let anybody go happily or easily. The forces of darkness hate the glory of God. They love the darkness and they want to keep us enslaved and captive so that we may worship them. They fight against God's redemption outside and inside the church. The forces of darkness say through Pharaoh, 'Who is this lord that we should obey him? We will not let you go and worship him.' (Exodus 5:2) But God will be glorified, and the only way that he can deliver us and redeem us from slavery is by bringing judgment on all that enslaves us.

Just as the Exodus is a rehearsal for the great Salvation, so the plagues of Egypt are a rehearsal for the final Judgment, because God has appointed Jesus Christ as the judge of the living and the dead, and has given all judgment into his hands. When the Lord Jesus Christ comes again with all his angels he will gather before him everybody who has ever lived, and as a shepherd separates the sheep from the goats he will separate all of us (Matthew 25:31-46). The sheep will go into eternal life and the goats will go away into eternal punishment, when he comes again with glory to judge both the living and the dead, whose kingdom shall have no end. And on that day every tongue will cry, 'Worthy is the Lamb, who was slain, to receive power and wealth and wisdom and strength and honour and glory and praise!' (Revelation 5:12)

So judgment and salvation go together. But even in judgment God is being gracious. He is being merciful, not just towards his own people but also towards his enemies. Before every plague the Lord God sends Moses to warn Pharaoh and the Egyptians, so that they too may repent and be redeemed, because even in judgment God has a missionary purpose. God says to Pharaoh. 'But I have raised you up for this very purpose, that I might show you my power and that my name might be proclaimed in all the earth.' (Exodus 9:16) Redemption, judgment – both display of the glory of God, until that day when every knee will bow before him. It is very important to notice that God treats his enemies with very great dignity, and we must too.

But Pharaoh hardens his heart, and God sends the angel of death in the final plague to take the first born of every house. However, he graciously gives his people this promise: they are to take a spotless lamb and kill it, and put the blood on the doorposts of their house, and every house that has the blood of the lamb on the doorpost the angel of death will pass over, because redemption now comes through the substitution of the blood of the lamb (Exodus12:1-13).

When Jesus came to be baptised by John the Baptist, John said, 'Look, the lamb of God, who takes away the sin of the world!' (John 1:29) We need to beware of anyone who removes substitution from the message of redemption. There is no redemption without substitution. It is all God's grace, it is God's sovereign power. It is God remembering his mercy to Abraham, God being faithful to his covenant. God fights for the Israelites and wins a mighty victory against the greatest power of the day.

When we turn to the New Testament we find that the grinding cruelty of slavery, which the people experienced in Egypt, is a shadow of the deeper and more vicious and immovable slavery, to sin and to death and to Satan himself. That is why Jesus' ministry was so full of conflict. The moment he was baptised he went into the wilderness and entered into mortal conflict with the evil one. So deep is God's love for us, so precious are we, that he puts forward his son to redeem us.

> *There is no redemption without substitution. It is all God's grace, it is God's sovereign power*

Study 2: The Presence of God

In his death and resurrection Jesus fights for us and defeats our enemies, and redeems us.

So the first question that Exodus answers is, 'What is redemption?' It is God acting to rescue us from slavery.

2. Why does God redeem us?

Why does God go to all this trouble? Exodus 24 is one of the most amazing and surprising passages in the entire Bible. God has rescued his people and he has brought them to the mountain (Mount Sinai), and now on this day God takes some of his friends and brings them up onto the mountain. God comes down, heaven opens, and God has a meal with his friends. They are allowed into heaven for a brief time. Everything in this chapter takes us back to God's purposes in Creation, and back to the blessing of God promised to Abraham. The reason that God redeems us is that he wants to be our God and us to be his people. He wants to share his glory with us so that we might enter into his glory. This is the reason for redemption – that he might dwell with us, that we might be together with him in communion and joy. In verse 1 God says, 'Come up to the Lord'. Seven times in this chapter he says, 'Come up'. He cannot come down because they are still sinful, and if he were to come down he would destroy them. So God keeps calling them up.

After the sacrifices we read these words, 'Moses and Aaron, Nadab and Abihu, and the seventy elders of Israel went up and saw the God of Israel. Under his feet was something like a pavement made of sapphire, clear as the sky itself. But God did not raise his hand against these leaders of the Israelites; they saw God, and they ate and drank.' (verses 9-11)

Don't you think that eating meals together can be one of the great and special things of life? My family lives 13,000 kilometres away from us – we are in Canada and they are in Australia. We meet every couple of years, when all the family will gather and sit down face to face, and eat and laugh and cry together.

In Exodus 24 God invites the leaders of the people he has rescued from slavery into his presence for a meal together. We know that no human can look on God and live. To show us how stunning this is, we see from verse 11 that God did not raise his hand

> *The reason that God redeems us is that he wants to be our God and us to be his people.*

against them – they saw God, and they ate and drank. We are not told what they saw – the language becomes very reserved and modest. We are not told about his appearance, only something about his surroundings – what the pavement was like under his feet, a piercing blue, a translucent and beautiful thing. But even those things are not actually described – we are told that under his feet was 'something like' a pavement, 'clear as the sky itself.' Yet somehow, in his grace and mercy, God withholds his hand from them, and they are allowed to eat and drink, and God allows himself to be seen with human eyes.

I don't think we go far enough as believers. We place a great emphasis on the forgiveness of sins, as is right, but forgiveness is not the final point, it's not the goal; we must not stop with the forgiveness of sins. Forgiveness leads to feasting. Freedom from sin leads to fellowship with God and one another. God frees us from our sins, not merely so that we may have a clean conscience, but so that we may sit down together and enjoy the presence and the face of God, and eat and drink with him and one another. The freedom of redemption is meant to lead to a close and abiding friendship with God, where we look on him as he shares with us. Do you not think that GAFCON is a little taste of this? With so many reunions with friends from around the world, friends we have not seen for many years, and singing the praises of God together, though we've come from very different places, and eating our meals together, are we not getting ready for the heavenly feast in the presence of God?

This is what the second half of Exodus is all about. From here on there are thirteen chapters devoted to the tabernacle – curtain rods and curtain rings and stitching and gold, and it is all so that God may come and dwell among his people. 'Then I will dwell among the Israelites and be their God. They will know that I am the Lord their God, who brought them out of Egypt so that I might dwell among them.' (Exodus 29:45,46) God wants to settle with us. He wants

> *God frees us from our sins, not merely so that we may have a clean conscience, but so that we may sit down together and enjoy the presence and the face of God, and eat and drink with him and one another*

Study 2: The Presence of God

to dwell with us. That is why he created us. God has made us to dwell with him, in true communion with himself and each other.

So this is the 'Why' of redemption. The whole point of the rescue is not just to free us, to show that God is Lord of all the earth, but that he may meet with us, and that we may enter into his glory and participate in his holiness. This is why in chapter 24 there is such an emphasis on the word of God. There can be neither friendship nor communion unless there is truthfulness between God and humans. In verse 3 we read that Moses came and told the people all the words and laws of the Lord, and later in that verse that the people responded, 'Everything the Lord has said we will do.' In verse 4 Moses wrote down everything the Lord had said. In verse 12 the Lord said to Moses, 'Come up to me on the mountain and stay here, and I will give you the tablets of stone, with the law and the commands I have written for their instruction.'

Let us go on a little pilgrimage now. Have you noticed, as you read through Exodus, that God tells Moses to write down what he says? This is the second time. God goes up on the mountain and gives Moses the two tablets, inscribed by the finger of God. (Exodus 31:18) We learn later that the tablets were the work of God, and the writing was the writing of God, engraved on the tablets. (Exodus 32:16) Moses comes down with two rocks on which the commandments of God are written. The commandments are God's work, and he wrote them on the rocks so that the words could not be changed. Moses wrote what God said and what God did, so that all Israel would be careful to do what is written. This is an essential part of redemption; the way of God with us, his people. This Word is not just a record of what believers in the past have struggled to understand. God wanted these words to be written down so that they would continue to have his authority. They would continue to be the instruments of redemption to bring us into friendship with him. As we read these words it is as though we are with the seventy on the mountain, hearing the words of God and having a meal with him.

Remember Satan's first

> *The whole point of the rescue is not just to free us ... but that he may meet with us, and that we may enter into his glory*

strategy in the Garden of Eden? It was to attack the word of God: 'Did God say?' (Genesis 3:1) And when Eve began to be caught into the snare, what was the first doctrine that Satan openly denied? It was the doctrine of judgment: 'You will not surely die.' (Genesis 3:4) And throughout the Old Testament whenever God's people turn away and forget God's word, they go after other gods. Whenever they turn back to God for revival and renewing, they turn back to his word written.

How will the Spirit of God revive and renew us? We must turn back to the words written, with hearts open and obedient. This is what Jesus believed. In all his arguments, what did Jesus appeal to? The word of God, 'it is written'. In all his decisions, what did Jesus appeal to? The Scriptures, 'it is written'. In John's gospel, when Jesus was arguing with the Pharisees, he says this: 'But since you do not believe what he [Moses] wrote, how are you going to believe what I say?' (John 5:47) We cannot take a different attitude to the writings of Moses and the words of Jesus. Both of them carry the power and authority of God, then and now. That is why the Scriptures remain eternally relevant. It is through these words that the Holy Spirit continues to revive and renew us.

One more point about the word of God. Just like forgiveness, we must not stop with the words of God. These words are not a stopping place, they are meant to lead us into a deeper and deeper relationship with him. They are meant to make us long for the great feast on that day, when we will take our place with Abraham and Isaac and Jacob in the kingdom of heaven, when we will see the table he has prepared for us, when we will enjoy the greatest, longest, most delicious feast, in fellowship with one another and face to face with God.

If there is any doubt that this is where we are going, consider the last paragraph in chapter 24. Moses goes up the mountain and into the cloud of God's presence covering the mountain. The glory of God immersed Moses and the top of the mountain. In verse 17 we read that God's glory looked like a consuming fire, but Moses was in there, sharing friendship with God for forty days and forty nights – and that is where we are going.

This is the goal of our salvation – not just forgiveness, not just freedom, but entering into God's glory. What is redemption? It is liberation from slavery by the great act of God. Why does God redeem us? It is so that we may become part of his glory, entering into fellowship with him face to face.

3. How does God redeem us?

He redeems us by the blood of the Covenant.

How is it possible that these men in Exodus 24 could be in the presence of God without perishing? It has to do with the blood of the covenant.

Before he goes up the mountain, Moses builds an altar just as God has commanded, with twelve pillars around it. He sacrifices one bull, which is completely burned on the altar. Then he takes another and nicely cooks it as a peace offering. Then he takes half the blood of the bull and splashes it on the altar; the other half he sprinkles over the people. We read in verse 8, 'Moses then took the blood, sprinkled it on the people and said, "This is the blood of the covenant that the Lord has made with you in accordance with all these words."'

These are very precious words to us as Christians. God is a God who makes and keeps covenant. The blood that is being thrown on the altar and the people shows that this is a matter of life and death, and it establishes us in a sacred relationship based on God's rescue.

Although God could have easily rescued his people from slavery, they could not have stood before him, nor could they have entered his glory, because of one thing – sin. We know that sin separates; we know that the wages of sin is death. The only way God can bring us into his presence is if our sins are taken away from us, and are paid for, and are covered. If you or I are to have a relationship with God, someone has to die for our sin – we cannot enter his glory as we are.

That is why Moses splashes the blood in two directions, first towards the altar, so that the right anger and punishment of God is turned aside, and then over all the people, like a huge covering of mercy. It is very graphic. Blood is the symbol of death; it's not just blood, but the symbol of a life

> *someone has to die for our sin – we cannot enter his glory as we are*

poured out. It shows something of what it takes for God to bring us into his presence, and it shows how seriously God takes his own glory. All the Old Testament sacrifices point forward to the day when Jesus himself, the Lamb of God, gave his life for us on the cross. On the night before Jesus gave himself over to death, he had Exodus 24 in mind. Matthew's gospel tells us this: 'Then he took the cup, gave thanks and offered it to them, saying, "Drink from it, all of you. This is my blood of the covenant, which is poured out for many for the forgiveness of sins. I tell you, I will not drink of this fruit of the vine from now on until that day when I drink it anew with you in my Father's kingdom."' (Matthew 26:27-29)

In saying this Jesus fulfils every Old Testament sacrifice. He opens a new covenant, not just with the blood of bulls and goats but with his own blood. (Hebrews 9:12) He gives a little glimpse of how we will sit down with him and eat and drink anew in the kingdom of God.

This is what we were made for. God has opened a way for us to enter in, through the blood of the covenant. Jesus shows us how determined God is to open the way for us, to draw us close to himself. This is not the cheap grace of tolerance and acceptance; this is the costly grace of redemption and sacrifice. The Son of God gave himself for us to redeem us from all wickedness, to purify for himself a people who are his very own, eager to do what is good. (Titus 2:14)

This is the shape of the gospel – Christ suffered once for all, the righteous for the unrighteous. Why? So that he might bring us to God. (1Peter 3:18) This was God's purpose when he made the world. This is God's purpose for our future in the new creation – to make us his people, in his place, in his presence.

Therefore hold fast to this redemption. The Bible is redemption-shaped. The gospel is a gospel of redemption. It is this which is at stake in our Communion today. If you take redemption out of the gospel, or replace it with tolerance or affirmation, there is no gospel, and we are lost. If we take redemption out of the gospel we lose any witness to the transforming grace of Jesus Christ. We lose the engine which makes us holy, the

> *This is not the cheap grace of tolerance and acceptance; this is the costly grace of redemption and sacrifice.*

Study 2: The Presence of God

forgiveness of our sins. We begin to treat our slave masters as if they are holy and good, and bow down to them. We lose the joy of our communion and the joy of entering the glory of God and being in his presence.

Let us rejoice in our redemption. Let us be a people of redemption. In the blood of Jesus Christ we have an eternal redemption. The song that we will sing in heaven is the song of the redeemed (Revelation 15:3), because God has made him to be our wisdom, our righteousness, our holiness and our redemption. (1 Corinthians 1:30)

Amen

Discussion Questions

1. *In this passage the covenant relationship between God and his people is expressed in blood and death. Is this easy or difficult for our culture to accept?*

2. *How is fellowship with God expressed in this passage? How should it be expressed in our Christian fellowships? How is it to be maintained?*

3. *What are the key themes concerning the presence of God that are highlighted in this teaching?*

Canon David Short has been rector of St. John's (Shaughnessy) Church in Vancouver, British Columbia since 1993. Born in Tanzania and raised in Africa and Sydney, Australia, he graduated from Moore Theological College with first class honours and was ordained priest in 1987. He has degrees from the University of Wollongong and Moore College in Australia, and also a Th.M from Regent College in Vancouver.

David is a recognized Bible teacher, expository preacher and trainer. He is a founder and now the Executive Director of the Artizo Institute, a Canadian initiative to identify and train young people who are gifted for pastoral ministry. He is a board member and theologian for the Anglican Network in Canada, a new ecclesial body upholding the orthodox and historic biblical faith in the face of the theological innovations of the Anglican Church of Canada. David was appointed an Honorary Canon of St Andrew's Cathedral in Sydney, Australia, in December 2008.

David and his wife, Bronwyn, have two boys, Benjamin and Joshua.

4. How is the presence of God experienced in the way in which he redeems us?

5. What are the marks of redemption that should characterize our daily discipleship?

6. How do we share our wonder at the costliness, the permanence and the transformative character of redemption, in a world that feels trapped by its past or its fate?

Study 3: The King of God

2 Samuel 7
God's Promise to David

¹ After the king was settled in his palace and the LORD had given him rest from all his enemies around him, ² he said to Nathan the prophet, "Here I am, living in a palace of cedar, while the ark of God remains in a tent."

³ Nathan replied to the king, "Whatever you have in mind, go ahead and do it, for the LORD is with you."

⁴ That night the word of the LORD came to Nathan, saying:

⁵ "Go and tell my servant David, 'This is what the LORD says: Are you the one to build me a house to dwell in? ⁶ I have not dwelt in a house from the day I brought the Israelites up out of Egypt to this day. I have been moving from place to place with a tent as my dwelling. ⁷ Wherever I have moved with all the Israelites, did I ever say to any of their rulers whom I commanded to shepherd my people Israel, "Why have you not built me a house of cedar?"'

⁸ "Now then, tell my servant David, 'This is what the LORD Almighty says: I took you from the pasture and from following the flock to be ruler over my people Israel. ⁹ I have been with you wherever you have gone, and I have cut off all your enemies from before you. Now I will make your name great, like the names of the greatest men of the earth. ¹⁰ And I will provide a place for my people Israel and will plant them so that they can have a home of their own and no longer be disturbed. Wicked people will not oppress them anymore, as they did at the beginning ¹¹ and have done ever since the time I appointed

2 Samuel 7
The King of God

The Revd Vaughan Roberts

A number of years ago I was on holiday in Indonesia. A friend of mine and I got into a taxi and there, at the front of the taxi, dangling just in front of the driver's eyes, was a strange looking object. My friend said to the taxi driver, 'What is that object?' And he said, 'Oh, that's easy, that's my God.' My friend said, 'Does your God speak to you?' and the taxi driver just laughed. It was laughable to think that this inanimate object could possibly speak to him. And my friend said to him, 'Our God speaks to us.'

It is an amazing privilege to expound the word of the living God. The Bible is living, and the living God speaks to us through it. This chapter, 2 Samuel chapter 7, is a wonderful chapter in which God tells us more about his rescue plan for our damaged world.

In Kings College Chapel, in Cambridge, a painting by Reubens of the infant Jesus hangs above the Lord's Table. In the early 1970s a vandal slashed into that priceless painting the letters IRA – Irish Republican Army, a terrorist organisation. It completely spoiled the painting. And yet the next day a simple sign was placed in front of the picture, which just said, 'It is believed that this masterpiece can be restored to its original condition.'

The Bible begins with a description of God's great masterpiece, his perfect creation: human beings made in the image of God, living in fellowship with him in a perfect world – God's people, in God's place, in God's presence. Then disaster struck: human beings rebelled against God and everything was spoiled. Human beings were banished from his presence – no longer his people, no longer in his place, no longer in his presence. And that is where the Bible could have ended. It is only because our God is a God of amazing grace that the Bible does not end at Genesis chapter 3. It's as if a great banner is placed above the devastation of Genesis 3: it says not just, 'It is believed', but rather, 'It is *guaranteed* that this masterpiece will be restored to its original condition.' The guarantee comes by divine covenant, divine promise. We saw it yesterday in Genesis chapter 12. You know there is only one gospel, one story of good news? It's there embryonically in Genesis 12, and then it's gradually fleshed out as

STUDY 3: THE KING OF GOD

leaders [a] over my people Israel. I will also give you rest from all your enemies.

"'The LORD declares to you that the LORD himself will establish a house for you: [12] *When your days are over and you rest with your fathers, I will raise up your offspring to succeed you, who will come from your own body, and I will establish his kingdom.* [13] *He is the one who will build a house for my Name, and I will establish the throne of his kingdom forever.* [14] *I will be his father, and he will be my son. When he does wrong, I will punish him with the rod of men, with floggings inflicted by men.* [15] *But my love will never be taken away from him, as I took it away from Saul, whom I removed from before you.* [16] *Your house and your kingdom will endure forever before me [b]; your throne will be established forever.'"*

[17] *Nathan reported to David all the words of this entire revelation.*

DAVID'S PRAYER

[18] *Then King David went in and sat before the LORD, and he said:*

"Who am I, O Sovereign LORD, and what is my family, that you have brought me this far? [19] *And as if this were not enough in your sight, O Sovereign LORD, you have also spoken about the future of the house of your servant. Is this your usual way of dealing with man, O Sovereign LORD?*

[20] *"What more can David say to you? For you know your servant, O Sovereign LORD.* [21] *For the sake of your word and according to your will, you have done this great thing and made it known to your servant.*

[22] *"How great you are, O Sovereign LORD! There is no one like you, and*

Study 3: The King of God

> there is no God but you, as we have heard with our own ears. ²³ And who is like your people Israel—the one nation on earth that God went out to redeem as a people for himself, and to make a name for himself, and to perform great and awesome wonders by driving out nations and their gods from before your people, whom you redeemed from Egypt? [c] ²⁴ You have established your people Israel as your very own forever, and you, O LORD, have become their God.
>
> ²⁵ "And now, LORD God, keep forever the promise you have made concerning your servant and his house. Do as you promised, ²⁶ so that your name will be great forever. Then men will say, 'The LORD Almighty is God over Israel!' And the house of your servant David will be established before you.
>
> ²⁷ "O LORD Almighty, God of Israel, you have revealed this to your servant, saying, 'I will build a house for you.' So your servant has found courage to offer you this prayer. ²⁸ O Sovereign LORD, you are God! Your words are trustworthy, and you have promised these good things to your servant. ²⁹ Now be pleased to bless the house of your servant, that it may continue forever in your sight; for you, O Sovereign LORD, have spoken, and with your blessing the house of your servant will be blessed forever."
>
> **Footnotes:**
> a 2 Samuel 7:11 Traditionally *judges*
> b 2 Samuel 7:16 Some Hebrew manuscripts and Septuagint; most Hebrew manuscripts *you*
> c Samuel 7:23 See Septuagint and 1 Chron. 17:21; Hebrew *wonders for your land and before your people, whom you redeemed from Egypt, from the nations and their gods.*

we go through the Old Testament until finally it's fulfilled in the Lord Jesus Christ. We saw yesterday [see previous study] how God acted in accordance with his promise, rescued the Israelites from slavery, gave them a great law and lived with them in the tabernacle, that symbol of his presence. Well, here in 2 Samuel chapter 7 we come to another great development in the saving purposes of God; he makes it clear that, when he intervenes to save the world, he will rule through a king.

We are increasingly cynical about leadership in our world today. We've seen too many leaders succumb to the temptations of corruption and egomania, more concerned to line their own pockets than to look after their people – there's a terrible example in Zimbabwe at the moment. But even the best leaders don't seem to be able to change very much; or at least if they do change things it doesn't seem to last for very long. And there's a crisis of leadership in the church also. As we look around, and recognise that we don't have the leaders we would long to have in many, many cases, then we think to ourselves, 'Wouldn't it be wonderful if God were to raise up a leader, someone who'd make a real difference, a leader after God's own heart who could change things so that they really stay changed?' But God says, 'Look up! That great leader has come! He is my King, and he will come again.'

It is that great King of God who is the theme of 2 Samuel chapter 7: he is the one through whom God will restore his masterpiece. As we look at this magnificent chapter we will notice three great truths about God's King: he is chosen by God, he is descended from David, and he is enthroned forever.

1. Chosen by God

First, God's king is chosen by God.

David, by this stage of 2 Samuel, has just been proclaimed king over all the people of Israel. He has established Jerusalem as his capital; he has brought the ark, that great symbol of the presence of God, into his capital city; and he has built a luxurious palace for himself to live in. Yet he senses that something isn't quite right, and so he says to Nathan the prophet, verse 2, 'Here I am, living in a palace of cedar, while the ark of God remains in a tent.' By now the tabernacle was centuries old; it would have been tatty and threadbare. We can imagine David saying to Nathan, 'It's not right, we should build a magnificent temple for God to live in.' Nathan encourages David to go ahead with whatever he has in mind; it seems wise and godly. But God's ways are not our ways and so God speaks to Nathan and makes it clear that David is not to be the one to build God a temple.

David's mistake was that he presumed to take the initiative.

Here is the great difference between Christianity and all human religions: human religions begin on earth with human beings deciding who God is and how we'll worship him, and it can never work. Why? Our brains are much too small and our hearts are far too sinful ever to come to a *true* knowledge of who God is and how we should worship him. Trying to decide these things ourselves makes for human religion, which begins with the initiative of human beings. By contrast, Christianity, the one true religion, begins with the initiative of God, when he says, 'This is what I'm like and this is how you are to worship me.' God takes the initiative.

I wonder whether you've noticed, from verse 8 onwards,

> *Christianity, the one true religion, begins with the initiative of God as God says, "This is what I'm like and this is how you're to worship me."*

Study 3: The King of God

how often the word 'I' comes? Thirteen times, in the next nine verses, 'I' or 'The Lord' is the subject. God takes the initiative; it had always been his intention that he would reign through a King. Even before the people entered the promised land, back in Deuteronomy 17, God made it clear to Moses that one day he would reign through a King. But when at last the people do ask for a king, they ask from all the wrong motivations: they ask in effect for a king instead of God, rather than a King under God. They want 'a king over us like all the other nations around us.' God does give them a king, Saul. But, he's not the King after God's own heart; he doesn't last for long.

Then God tells Samuel to go to Jesse's household, and the older boys are presented to Samuel one by one. They're strapping lads, they look excellent king material, but each time God says, 'No, he's not the one; no, he's not the one; no, he's not the one.' Samuel begins to get worried and he says, 'Are these all your sons?', and Jesse says, 'Oh, there's one other, the boy, the shepherd boy, he's looking after the sheep.' No one had thought of him, but it was David who was God's chosen king. God takes the initiative and, in verse 8 of our passage, he reminds David, 'I took you from the pasture and from following the flock to be ruler over my people Israel.'

Just as, in the past, it was God's initiative to establish David as king, so in the future it will be God's initiative to raise up the future King, through whom all God's promises will be fulfilled forever. So, in verse 12, God says, 'I will establish his kingdom', and in verse 14, 'I will be his father, and he shall be my son.' God's King does not establish himself by political scheming or by military victory, he is not elected by democratic vote: he is chosen by God. And about a thousand years after this promise, when the Lord Jesus went into the desert to be baptised by his cousin, John, a great voice boomed from Heaven: 'This is my Son, whom I love; with him I am well pleased.' (Matthew 3:17), God was saying, 'He is the one, this is the one.'

The Lord Jesus has more

...although its legitimacy was questioned, his birth, in an obscure village in Israel, has split time in two: we speak of BC and AD. Who was this remarkable man?

Study 3: The King of God

websites devoted to him than Madonna and Tiger Woods put together; he's been in more movies than James Bond; he never wrote a book, yet he's the hero of history's number one bestseller; he never travelled as an adult outside the country of his birth, yet he has more followers worldwide today than anyone else, living or dead. And although its legitimacy was questioned, his birth, in an obscure village in Israel, has split time in two: we speak of BC and AD. Who was this remarkable man? God says, 'He is my son, he is my chosen King. He is the one.' God testified by that voice at the baptism; God testified again by that voice at the transfiguration (Luke 9:35); God testified through the miracles; God testified most supremely to his eternal son by raising him from the dead. Jesus is the chosen one, God's King.

When I was a student we had a mission; we were asked to invite our friends to hear the good news of Jesus Christ, and I knocked on the door of all my friends. One of my friends was a Sikh. He was a very mild man and I thought there'd be no problem. I knocked on the door, he opened it, very friendly, and then I said, 'I'm just inviting you to come to a Christian talk because we'd love all our friends to hear the good news about Jesus Christ.' This mild man changed completely! He said, 'How dare you invite me to hear about Jesus! You may have chosen him as your way to God, you may have chosen him as your king, but I've chosen to follow a very different path to life and it is extremely arrogant of you to invite me to hear about Jesus, as if your chosen way is the best chosen way!'

And of course, if Christianity begins on earth with human beings choosing Jesus as our King, then it *is* the height of arrogance to claim that my choice, my King, is somehow better than yours. But, Christianity does not begin on earth, with me choosing Jesus as my King. It begins in Heaven, with God sending down his eternal son. Jesus is not just my King, he's God's King. He's not just the one I've chosen to follow, he's the one God has chosen to reign. There is one Jesus Christ, one Lord, one Saviour, one King.

John Stott once said, 'We

> *"We may speak of Alexander the Great and Charles the Great and Napoleon the Great, but not Jesus the Great. Jesus is not the great, Jesus is the only. Our place is on our faces before him in worship."*

Study 3: The King of God

may speak of Alexander the Great and Charles the Great and Napoleon the Great, but not Jesus the Great. Jesus is not the great, Jesus is the only. Our place is on our faces before him in worship.' God's King is chosen by God.

2. Descended from David

Here is the second great truth from this passage: God's King is descended from David. In this chapter we have one of the great divine promises, often called the Davidic Covenant. But we shouldn't see it so much as a separate promise from God, but rather as an expansion of the earlier promise, the covenant with Abraham. Remember, there's one gospel, embryonic with Abraham and then gradually fleshed out. Here's one of the examples of passages in the Old Testament where it's fleshed out, before being fulfilled in Jesus Christ. In this promise we have echoes of the promise to Abraham. God said to Abraham, 'I will make your name great', and 'I will give you a place to live in', and sure enough we have echoes of those promises here: in verse 9 God says, 'I will make your name great', and in verse 10 he says, 'I will provide a place for my people'. And so the question comes, 'This great promise to Abraham, filled out a bit to David, when will it be fulfilled?' God says, in verse 12, 'When your days are over and you rest with your fathers, I will raise up your offspring to succeed you, who will come from your own body, and I will establish his kingdom. He is the one who will build a house for my Name, and I will establish the throne of his kingdom for ever.'

Remember, there's one gospel, embryonic with Abraham, gradually fleshed out ... in the Old Testament before it's fulfilled in Jesus Christ.

That word 'house' has a double meaning in English; it has the same double meaning in Hebrew. It can mean a home, but it can also mean a dynasty. So, at the end of verse 11 God is saying, 'David, you wanted to build a house, a home, for me, but I'm going to build a house, a dynasty, for *you*.' From now on we wonder, 'Who is this great king of David's line, who will build a house for God, and through whom all God's promises will be fulfilled?' We read on in the Bible and we think, 'Well, surely it's Solomon.' Solomon is a great son of David, and in many ways a greater king than David. He is the one who

Study 3: The King of God

builds the temple that God is to live in. 'Now at last,' we think, 'we have the promises fulfilled: God's people, in God's place, in God's presence.' But then, of course, Solomon sins. He marries many foreign wives, and his sin is not simply sexual; it is also spiritual, because those foreign wives bring their foreign gods with them and corrupt the nation into idolatry. And so judgement must come: the kingdom divides after Solomon dies. The kings of Judah, that tiny nation of Judah, are still of the line of David, but none of those kings even approaches the great king Solomon; even the better ones are still corrupted by idolatry. Then comes God's definitive judgement: the Babylonians destroy the city of Jerusalem and that's the end of the Davidic line. It seems as if there's little hope, but while Israel's history declares the failure of Israel, God's prophets point to the future of Israel. It's all on the basis of this promise: God has promised that there will be a king of the line of David, and no matter how miserable things are in the history of Israel, God will fulfil his promise. So God says to Isaiah, in some very familiar words, 'For to us a child is born, to us a son is given, and the government will be on his shoulders .... He will reign on David's throne and over his kingdom' (Isaiah 9:6,7). David himself speaks of the coming King in the verse of the Old Testament that is quoted in the New Testament more than any other, Psalm 110, verse 1: 'The Lord says to my Lord: "Sit at my right hand until I make your enemies a footstall for your feet."' And then, as the great King Jesus rode in to this city of Jerusalem on a donkey, the people realised the truth, and they cried out, 'Hosanna to the Son of David!' (Matthew 21:9)

At the heart of our divisions in the Anglican Communion is a difference in our understandings of Scripture.

Do you know how the first book of the New Testament begins? Matthew begins his gospel with a long genealogy, and most of us quickly flick over those pages, finding them rather dull and boring, and assuming they have nothing to say to us. But actually they are very significant indeed: they are saying that Jesus is the one who fulfils all that has come before. Matthew 1:1 says, 'A record of the genealogy of Jesus Christ the son of David, the son of Abraham'. In other words, Matthew is telling us, right at the

Study 3: The King of God

beginning, 'This is the one; he's the one who has come in fulfilment of all the Old Testament promises.' The whole Bible is about Jesus Christ.

Turning to the present day, at the heart of our divisions in the Anglican Communion is a difference in our understandings of Scripture. This means that some people will say to us, 'You claim the authority of the Bible, and we agree, the Bible is very important indeed, but you must recognise that the Bible speaks with many different voices. It's a collection of books that point in different directions, so you cannot simplistically claim, 'The Bible says...'. More honestly you should say, 'One part of the Bible seems to say..., but another part of the Bible might seem to say something different.'" Well, it's true that we don't believe about the Bible what Muslims believe about the Koran: we don't believe it was just dictated by God from Heaven, with no human involvement at all. It is a human book, containing sixty-six different books by forty different human authors, and these different books bear the marks of the different human authors, and of the different times and circumstances in which they wrote. It's a human book but it is also divine, because God the Holy Spirit ensured that those different human authors, writing at different times in history, wrote exactly what he wanted them to write. So, while on the one hand it *is* a human book, with many different authors and many different books, on the other hand, supremely, it is one book with one great divine author and one over-arching subject: God's plan to save the world through his son, his King, the Lord Jesus Christ. So, in the Old Testament we have Christ promised, and in the New Testament Christ proclaimed. The whole of the Old Testament points to him. This is true of the passages familiar from carol services, the obvious prophecies, but it's true of all the history as well. As we look at Great King David we see just a model, a pattern, a shadow, of Great David's Greater Son, the Great King Jesus, who is God's King, chosen by God, descended from David.

> *So, while on the one hand it is a human book, with many different authors and many different books, on the other hand, supremely, it is one book with one great divine author and one over-arching subject*

Study 3: The King of God

3. Enthroned forever

Third and finally: God's King is enthroned forever. Look at verse 13. God says, 'He is the one who will build a house for my Name, and I will establish the throne of his kingdom for ever.' God's promise to David, that he is going to raise up a great King from his descendents, is absolutely secure, it cannot be broken. It cannot be broken by death. God makes it clear in verse 12 that David will die: 'When your days are over and you rest with your fathers, I will raise up your offspring to succeed you'. Death cannot spoil or end God's promise. His promise cannot be broken by death and, more than that, it cannot be broken by sin – see verse 14, 'I will be his father, and he shall be by son. When he does wrong, I will punish him with the rod of men, with floggings inflicted by men. But my love will never be taken away from him, as I took it away from Saul'. It's true that individual kings of David's line will sin, and individual kings of David's line will be disciplined by God – Solomon is an example. But their sin will not cancel God's great commitment that a king of David's line will reign forever. This promise cannot be broken by death or sin, and it cannot be broken by time – see verse 16, 'Your house and your kingdom shall endure for ever before me; your throne shall be established for ever.'

> *This promise can't be broken by death, or sin, or time: "Your house and your kingdom shall endure forever before me; your throne shall be established for ever."*

David, God's great king, died. Solomon died. All those other kings of the line of David, right up to the exile, they died too. But the prophets pointed to a King who would never die. Isaiah says, 'He will reign on David's throne and over his kingdom ... from that time on and for ever.' Then at last the Lord Jesus came. He began to preach, and what was his message? 'The time has come.' In other words, 'This is the moment you've been waiting for, for generations. The time has come; the kingdom of God is at hand.' And why is the kingdom of God at hand? Because the King has come.

Jesus said to the disciples, 'Who do you say I am?' and it was Simon, Simon Peter, who finally said, 'You are the Christ, the Son of the living God.' (Matthew 16:16) In other words, 'You are

Study 3: The King of God

the one prophesied in 2 Samuel chapter 7.' And the Lord Jesus said to him, '... you are Peter, and on this rock I will build my church ...' (Matthew 16:18). 'I will build my church.' Do you realise, that that is 2 Samuel language? In 2 Samuel chapter 7 God said that this coming King would 'build a house for my Name'. Well, Solomon did build a temple in Jerusalem, for Israel, but the Lord Jesus Christ is now building a much greater temple, his Church, which he builds from all nations. Later on, in his epistle, Peter wrote, 'As you come to him, the living Stone – rejected by men but chosen by God and precious to him – you also, like living stones, are being built into a spiritual house ...' (1 Peter 2:4,5). Have you ever thought that there are no holy places today, no place where God is especially present on earth? We don't have to go to a special building to meet with God. There are no holy buildings. But there *are* holy people, because he lives within us, his multi-racial Church.

Straight after Peter's recognition of Jesus as the Christ, Matthew tells us, the Lord Jesus 'began to explain to his disciples that he must ... suffer many things ... be killed and on the third day be raised to life.' (Matthew 16:21) Sure enough, he was arrested, he was crucified. He didn't look much like a king as he hung there in agony on the cross, but the Old Testament prophets had said he had to die. For this coming King would be a suffering servant, who would take upon himself the sin of the world. His friends buried him in a tomb, but God raised him to a throne. As Peter proclaimed on the day of Pentecost, '... let all Israel be assured of this: God has made this Jesus, whom you crucified, both Lord and Christ.' (Acts 2:36) Jesus died, he was raised, he ascended, and he is now seated at the right hand of God his Father in Heaven. To a world that is longing for proper leadership in the world and in the Church, God says, 'Look up! Jesus is my risen King! He's already enthroned at my right hand.'

For us today there's a real debate going on: where should true authority lie in the Anglican Communion? Who is our leader? Where is our leader? There

> *To a world that is longing for proper leadership in the world and in the Church, God says, "Look up! Jesus is my risen King! He's already enthroned at my right hand."*

Study 3: The King of God

are important discussions there, but let us never forget that our ultimate leader is not in Canterbury, nor in Kampala, nor Lagos nor anywhere else in the world. Our leader is in Heaven, seated at the right hand of God: Jesus Christ is Lord, he is God's King, chosen by God, descended from David, and enthroned for ever.

4. How do these great truths apply to us today?

4.1 We should be humble people

For a start, surely, we should be humble people. Louis XIV of France decreed that, at his funeral, the only source of light in Notre Dame Cathedral in Paris should come from a single candle, placed on his coffin, to give the impression that all the light in the world emanated from him. But on that solemn occasion the court preacher, Massillon, got up to preach the sermon, and as he passed the coffin on his way to the pulpit, he snuffed out the candle. He then began to preach, saying, 'Only God is great! Only God is great!'

This is a very significant time in the Anglican Communion. Dare I say it, it is a very significant time in the history of the Christian Church. It is a time that calls for decisive action and courageous leadership, and it may well be that in years to come people will look back to this conference as a decisive moment. And that's a great opportunity that we must not duck. But there is a great danger attached. We have the possibility of making history. But the danger is that we begin to think we're really rather special. This is always a danger for anyone in leadership. It is a danger for bishops and archbishops, for rectors, for anyone in a position of responsibility. In England there's something not right about the way we refer to our bishop's home as a palace; we call his chair in the cathedral a throne, and we put a mitre on his head and urge him to wear purple, the imperial colour. It was the apostle Paul who wrote, '... we do not preach ourselves, but Jesus Christ as Lord, and ourselves as your servants for Jesus' sake.' (2 Corinthians 4:5) There is only *one* King, so we should be humble people.

> *Much is made of the fact that he is our saviour (which, of course, is gloriously true), but very little is said about the fact that he is also the Lord who must be obeyed.*

Study 3: The King of God

Discussion Questions

Introductory questions: Can you give an example, from your culture or your experience, of the idea that there are many paths to salvation? Why is this idea attractive?

1. *In this passage what is the difference between David's aspirations and God's promises, and how are they both fulfilled?*

2. *What are the key themes, concerning Jesus as the future king of David's line, that are highlighted in this teaching?*

4.2 We should be obedient people

Next, of course, we should be obedient people. Jesus is a king, and kings must be obeyed. There's a kind of religion that gives the impression that what Jesus is doing is just making us feel nice and warm about ourselves. Much is made of the fact that he is our saviour (which, of course, is gloriously true), but very little is said about the fact that he is also the Lord who must be obeyed.

This conference has come about because of a crisis in our Anglican Communion, a crisis caused by some who have refused to obey the King and refused to submit to his standards in Scripture. But before we call on others to repent, as sadly we must, we ourselves must repent of our hypocrisy, of our moral compromise, of the many ways in which we, as individuals and as groups within our churches, have not submitted to this great King. We must be obedient people.

4.3 We should be evangelistic people

At my school there was a map on the wall – it must have been forty years out of date. It was one of those old maps which showed the British Empire in pink. In those days the British Empire seemed to dominate quite a lot of the world, but not any more. Many people, nowadays, seem to have in their heads a kind of religious map, in which the world is divided up between the domain of Christ, the domain of Allah, the domain of Krishna and the other Hindu gods, the domain of Hinduism, the domain of Communism .... But the Bible says, 'No, there is one God, there is one Lord Jesus Christ, and he reigns over the Middle East, he reigns over India, he reigns over China and the whole of Asia, he reigns over Africa, he reigns over Europe, he reigns over North America, he reigns over South America!' Jesus Christ is Lord of all, and our great task is to tell the world. We cannot have a narrow concern simply for the purity of the Church of God – though this must be a concern. We must have a passionate concern to tell the world that Jesus Christ is King.

4.4 We must be hopeful people

We must be humble, obedient, evangelistic and – finally, as we close – we must be hopeful people, *because* Jesus Christ is King. It is easy to be overwhelmed with despair as we look around at all the problems in the world: the AIDS epidemic, the environmental crisis, the rise of Islam. It's easy too to be overwhelmed with despair

3. Read Matthew 1:1 and Isaiah 9:6-7. In the light of the fact that Jesus is the divine fulfilment of the Davidic kingship:

a. what makes Christianity different from all other religions?

b. who is our ultimate leader in our churches?

c. what is the role of human leaders in our churches?

4. What will it mean in practice for us to respond to Jesus the king in our churches and in our personal lives:

a. With humility?

b. With obedience?

c. With evangelism?

d. With hope?

Study 3: The King of God

sometimes as we look at the situations in our Anglican Communion, or in our churches at home. But, as we begin to look around, it's as if God taps us on the shoulder and says, 'Look up! Look up!'

I love the book of Revelation. Before those awesome, sometimes terrifying visions of all that's going to happen between the ascension of the Lord Jesus and his return, John has one prior vision: he looks up and sees 'a lamb, looking as if it had been slain, standing in the centre of the throne'. (Revelation 5:6) It's as if God is saying, 'Before you can cope with the awful reality of a fallen world still in rebellion against me, you need to remember that Jesus Christ is Lord, and you need to see all that happens in the world through the spectacles of that vision.' There's a throne in Heaven, and it is not empty: Jesus Christ is sitting on it. And we need to look to him, to ask him to help us to be faithful to him, whatever the cost, as we serve him in this world, and as we look forward to the great day when he comes again, when every knee will bow and every tongue will confess that Jesus Christ is Lord, to the glory of God the Father (Philippians 2:10,11), that great day when his perfect masterpiece will be not just restored, but even better.

May God bring great glory to himself through his King, Jesus.

Amen.

Vaughan Roberts is the Rector of St Ebbe's Church, Oxford. Vaughan studied law at Cambridge University before a brief spell doing student ministry in South Africa. Since 1991 he has been on the staff of St Ebbe's Church, Oxford, where he is now Senior Pastor. Vaughan is a founding trustee of '9:38', which encourages people to consider full-time gospel ministry, and is a council member of Reform, a network of churches and individuals within the Church of England, which is committed to the reform of ourselves, our congregation and our world by the gospel. He is also on the leadership team of The Proclamation Trust, an organisation that aims to teach the Bible to preachers, in order that they may in turn teach it to others.

In his spare time he writes books and plays cricket, tennis and golf.

Study 4: The Son of God

Luke 24
The Son of God

Bishop Dr Michael Fape

Introduction

We thank God for the setting of our Bible Expositions. Today we are looking at the Son of God, who is the fulfilment of the promises made to Abraham in Genesis 12: he is the Lamb of God who takes away the sin of the world by the shedding of his blood, thereby establishing the new covenant that is prefigured in Exodus 24, and he is the King from the Davidic dynasty, whose throne will last forever, the perfect King anticipated in 2 Samuel 7.

The GAFCON conference is concerned mainly with the desire to go back to the Scriptures, to reclaim the foundations of Anglicanism which have been corrupted. Certainly, the centre no longer holds; things have fallen apart. There are members of our Anglican Communion who have removed the ancient landmarks, or boundary stones, which ought not to be removed. They have acted in defiant rejection of the Scripture which says, 'Do not move an ancient boundary stone set up by your forefathers' (Proverbs 22:28).

LUKE 24

THE RESURRECTION

¹*On the first day of the week, very early in the morning, the women took the spices they had prepared and went to the tomb.* ²*They found the stone rolled away from the tomb,* ³*but when they entered, they did not find the body of the Lord Jesus.* ⁴*While they were wondering about this, suddenly two men in clothes that gleamed like lightning stood beside them.* ⁵*In their fright the women bowed down with their faces to the ground, but the men said to them, "Why do you look for the living among the dead?* ⁶*He is not here; he has risen! Remember how he told you, while he was still with you in Galilee:* ⁷*'The Son of Man must be delivered into the hands of sinful men, be crucified and on the third day be raised again.'"* ⁸*Then they remembered his words.*

⁹*When they came back from the tomb, they told all these things to the Eleven and to all the others.* ¹⁰*It was Mary Magdalene, Joanna, Mary the mother of James, and the others with them who told this to the apostles.* ¹¹*But they did not believe the women, because their words seemed to them like nonsense.* ¹²*Peter, however, got up and ran to the tomb. Bending over, he saw the strips of linen lying by themselves, and he went away, wondering to himself what had happened.*

ON THE ROAD TO EMMAUS

¹³*Now that same day two of them were going to a village called Emmaus, about seven miles[a] from Jerusalem.* ¹⁴*They were talking with each other about everything that had happened.* ¹⁵*As they talked and*

Study 4: The Son of God

> *discussed these things with each other, Jesus himself came up and walked along with them; ¹⁶but they were kept from recognizing him.*
>
> *¹⁷He asked them, "What are you discussing together as you walk along?"*
> *They stood still, their faces downcast. ¹⁸One of them, named Cleopas, asked him, "Are you only a visitor to Jerusalem and do not know the things that have happened there in these days?"*
>
> *¹⁹ "What things?" he asked.*
> *"About Jesus of Nazareth," they replied. "He was a prophet, powerful in word and deed before God and all the people. ²⁰The chief priests and our rulers handed him over to be sentenced to death, and they crucified him; ²¹but we had hoped that he was the one who was going to redeem Israel. And what is more, it is the third day since all this took place. ²²In addition, some of our women amazed us. They went to the tomb early this morning ²³but didn't find his body. They came and told us that they had seen a vision of angels, who said he was alive. ²⁴Then some of our companions went to the tomb and found it just as the women had said, but him they did not see."*
>
> *²⁵He said to them, "How foolish you are, and how slow of heart to believe all that the prophets have spoken! ²⁶Did not the Christ[b] have to suffer these things and then enter his glory?" ²⁷And beginning with Moses and all the Prophets, he explained to them what was said in all the Scriptures concerning himself.*

The purpose of GAFCON is to proffer an answer to the age-old question of the Psalmist, 'When the foundations are being destroyed, what can the righteous do?' (Psalm 11:3). Yes, it may seem as if the foundations of Anglicanism have been destroyed by revisionism, but through all the ages God has always preserved a remnant, and now this remnant will recover the foundations of authentic Anglicanism. And God will restore the years that the locusts – the swarming locust, the crawling locust, the consuming locust, the chewing locust – have eaten (Joel 2:25).

There are some basic fundamental truths about Anglicanism which must be rediscovered and reaffirmed in every generation. These could be seen as the non-negotiable trade marks of authentic Anglicanism. Again, we thank God for the settings of our Bible Expositions. The context of Luke 24 undoubtedly provides great opportunities to appreciate the non-negotiable trade marks of authentic Anglicanism, as we travel this road of faith together. We are at this Conference for the defence of 'the faith that was once for all entrusted to the saints', to use the words of Jude (Jude verse 3). What is the content of this faith? The content is the historical and theological indispensability of the life, death and bodily resurrection from the dead of Jesus Christ. However, the resurrection event is the central thrust of Luke 24, an event that took place the third day after Jesus had been crucified, had died and been buried. This bodily resurrection resulted in the amazing story of the empty tomb, which authenticates Christ's absolute power over sin, death and the grave.

2. Luke 24:1-12

From Luke 24:1-12, it is apparent that those who went to the tomb to re-anoint or re-embalm the body of Christ had got it wrong. Christ himself had predicted the events of his death and resurrection many times before they actually happened (e.g. Mark 10:32-34). This was a simple truth, but for the disciples it was hard to believe. This is why Paul had to devote a whole chapter of one of his epistles to clarify this matter in the early Church (1 Corinthians 15:1ff). The event of the bodily resurrection of Christ is central to our faith as Anglicans; without it our faith is futile (1 Corinthians 15:12-19). Little wonder that each of the three Creeds affirms the truth of the actual death, burial and bodily resurrection of Jesus Christ.

> ^{28}As they approached the village to which they were going, Jesus acted as if he were going farther. ^{29}But they urged him strongly, "Stay with us, for it is nearly evening; the day is almost over." So he went in to stay with them.
>
> ^{30}When he was at the table with them, he took bread, gave thanks, broke it and began to give it to them. ^{31}Then their eyes were opened and they recognized him, and he disappeared from their sight. ^{32}They asked each other, "Were not our hearts burning within us while he talked with us on the road and opened the Scriptures to us?"
>
> ^{33}They got up and returned at once to Jerusalem. There they found the Eleven and those with them, assembled together ^{34}and saying, "It is true! The Lord has risen and has appeared to Simon." ^{35}Then the two told what had happened on the way, and how Jesus was recognized by them when he broke the bread.
>
> **JESUS APPEARS TO THE DISCIPLES**
> ^{36}While they were still talking about this, Jesus himself stood among them and said to them, "Peace be with you."
>
> ^{37}They were startled and frightened, thinking they saw a ghost. ^{38}He said to them, "Why are you troubled, and why do doubts rise in your minds? ^{39}Look at my hands and my feet. It is I myself! Touch me and see; a ghost does not have flesh and bones, as you see I have."
>
> ^{40}When he had said this, he showed them his hands and feet. ^{41}And while

Study 4: The Son of God

they still did not believe it because of joy and amazement, he asked them, "Do you have anything here to eat?" ⁴²They gave him a piece of broiled fish, ⁴³and he took it and ate it in their presence.

⁴⁴He said to them, "This is what I told you while I was still with you: Everything must be fulfilled that is written about me in the Law of Moses, the Prophets and the Psalms."

⁴⁵Then he opened their minds so they could understand the Scriptures. ⁴⁶He told them, "This is what is written: The Christ will suffer and rise from the dead on the third day, ⁴⁷and repentance and forgiveness of sins will be preached in his name to all nations, beginning at Jerusalem. ⁴⁸You are witnesses of these things. ⁴⁹I am going to send you what my Father has promised; but stay in the city until you have been clothed with power from on high."

The Ascension

⁵⁰When he had led them out to the vicinity of Bethany, he lifted up his hands and blessed them. ⁵¹While he was blessing them, he left them and was taken up into heaven. ⁵²Then they worshipped him and returned to Jerusalem with great joy. ⁵³And they stayed continually at the temple, praising God.

Footnotes:
a. Luke 24:13 Greek *sixty stadia* (about 11 kilometers)
b. Luke 24:26 Or *Messiah*; also in verse 46

Certainly, those who went to the tomb were sincere lovers of Christ. In fact their level of devotion to him was great, which was why they were going to the tomb. These were zealous followers, but their minds were darkened, because they had not grasped the profundity of Christ's teaching. Brethren, it is not enough to be zealous in our claims to be Anglicans if we are not totally rooted in the truths of the Scriptures. Some of us are like clouds without rain (Jude verse 12). If only those women had known the truth, they would not have been looking for 'the living among the dead' (Luke 24:5).

Brethren, just as Christ predicted his death and resurrection, he also predicted that there would be turbulent times for the Church – this was at Caesarea Philippi, just after Peter had made his Spirit-inspired confession that Jesus was the Christ. Responding to this confession, Christ declares, 'And I tell you that you are Peter, and on this rock I will build my church, and the gates of Hades will not overcome it' (Matthew 16:18). Regardless of the turbulent times we are passing through, the forces of darkness cannot overcome the Church of God. If we do all believe that it is the Church that Christ has redeemed with his blood, then 'Let us hold unswervingly to the hope

Study 4: The Son of God

we profess, for he who promised is faithful' (Hebrews 10:23).

The truth of the gospel is too simple to be believed by those who have not really encountered the resurrected Christ. When the women who went to the tomb came back and reported to the Apostles what they had seen, their report seemed like idle tales, or nonsense (Luke 24:10-11). In other words, Peter and his friends at first disbelieved the resurrection of Christ. Commenting on the simplicity of the truth of the gospel, Paul writes, 'For the message of the cross is foolishness to those who are perishing, but to us who are being saved it is the power of God' (1 Corinthians 1:18).

If there are those who are denying the truth of the gospel today, you now know the reason. It is simply because either they have not had a genuine encounter with the risen Christ or, like a living sacrifice, they have crawled away from the altar, they have not been regularly presenting their bodies to God as living sacrifices (Romans 12:1-2). That is why the call to them to return from the path that leads to destruction is nothing more than idle tales, or nonsense! Yes, to them holding on to the faith once delivered to the saints is a mark of an uncivilised and uneducated mind!

The Anglican Communion prides itself on being a body that brings together those who are committed to the orthodoxy of the Scriptures. That is why Article VI (of the Thirty-nine Articles), which upholds the Scriptures as containing everything that is necessary for our salvation, is absolutely central to authentic Anglicanism. This truth is being demonstrated here, now, as we see the Church, the assembly of the redeemed people of God, gathered around the word of God. In our gathering, we are enabled and energised to witness by the Spirit of God, who sanctifies us by the truth made manifest in his word, because his word is truth (John 17:17).

It is not enough to be zealous in our claims to be Anglicans if we are not totally rooted in the truths of the Scriptures.

3. Luke 24:13-24

Shortly after the disciples had received the report of the resurrection of Christ, which they had thought to be an idle tale, two of them made a journey to Emmaus, and Luke 24: 13-24 tells us of their bewilderment and

Study 4: The Son of God

frustration.

There are three points to note here. First, these two disciples were like-minded, which made it possible for them to have a discussion. This is the truth emphasised by Amos when he writes, 'Do two walk together unless they have agreed to do so?' (Amos 3:3, cf. Prov. 27:17). Second, they had a common subject matter, they both wanted to talk about Jesus. Though they had no clue to the problem of the empty tomb, yet they could not set aside the matters of Christ's life, ministry, death and resurrection. Third, because Christ was the subject of their discussion, he came 'on board' with them. This is the truth contained in the Scripture, 'For where two or three come together in my name, there am I with them' (Matthew 18:20).

Brethren, for those of us who are here, are *we* like-minded, intending to reaffirm the centrality of the Scriptures as the basis for Anglicanism? In other words, is it our aim to lift up the gospel of Christ, and to believe the Bible? Do we take the Bible as the single undivided Scripture of the Old and New Testaments, which contains all that is required for our salvation, and also for our sustenance as believers? Then Christ is certainly here to travel with us, as we seek to defend the faith that was once delivered to us! Yes, I am fully persuaded that Christ is here, and that he will guide us in every one of our programmes, watching to protect us from ravenous wolves (Psalm 32:8).

> *Do we take the Bible as the single undivided Scripture of the Old and New Testaments, which contains all that is required for our salvation, and also for our sustenance as believers?*

Returning to Luke's narrative, Christ has now become the silent listener to the conversation between the two disciples. However, he did not disclose his identity to them (verse 16). Why would Christ keep his identity hidden from those who so desperately desired to see him? Perhaps, to judge from his question to them in verse 17, he wanted to know the level of their commitment. It is true that the two disciples were talking about Jesus Christ, but were they really in love with him? From what is said in verses 18-24, it becomes very clear that the two disciples *were* in love with Christ. It is also clear that they were convinced about his mission to the world, and so they were able to give a reason for the hope they had had (1 Peter 3:15).

Again, my beloved, please permit me to pose the question: 'Why are you here?' Are you persuaded about the cause we are championing, here at GAFCON, or are you an ordinary emissary? If you are persuaded about the cause of GAFCON, then be prepared to give the reason for your hope in the Son of God. We are Anglicans not simply because we have joined a denomination. Being Anglican is synonymous with being among the redeemed people of God, whose faith is rooted in the undiluted message of the gospel.

4. Luke 24:25-27, 44-47

In the next two passages, verses 25-27 and 44-47, Christ demonstrated the supreme authority of the Scriptures. Having established a genuine personal relationship with the disciples, joining them as they walked to Emmaus, he expounded the Scriptures to them, enlightening the eyes of their heart and banishing the dullness of their understanding. Earlier, in their state of utter frustration and disappointment, the disciples had thought that Christ had come to be an earthly Messiah, to save Israel from the oppressive power of their captors (verse 21). But Christ took time to explain the Scriptures to them, redefining the global concept of his Messianic mission. There are three points to be noted here, in the light of the earlier three expositions [see previous studies].

First, God's promise in Genesis 12 – that he would make Abraham into a great nation, and that in him all the families of the earth would be blessed – goes beyond the single nation of Israel. While we acknowledge the significant role played by the people of Israel in God's agenda, on account of his choice of Abraham, yet the blessings accruing from this choice go beyond those who are Abraham's physical descendents. (This is made very clear in Galatians 3:13-14.) The promise of Genesis 12 finds fulfilment in the coming of Christ, who was born under the law to redeem those under the curse of the law, so that the promise of Abraham becoming a blessing and the father of many nations might be fulfilled. Christ, having redeemed us from

Study 4: The Son of God

the curse of the law, has imputed to us the blessings of Abraham, since we are now sons and daughters by adoption. There is an echo, here, of the Exodus – a crossing over from slavery to freedom, and from being under a curse to being blessed. However, only those who are saved by faith in Christ are sons and daughters of Abraham, and these are people are from all nations, tribes and languages. This is how, through Abraham, all the families of the earth are blessed.

Second, the salvation by faith of these sons of Abraham, and their incorporation into Christ, is through the shed blood of the cross at Calvary, a redemptive event which was anticipated in Exodus 24. Indeed, without the shedding of blood there is no remission of sin. As Christ expounded the Scriptures to the disciples, saying, 'Did not the Christ have to suffer these things ...', he demonstrated that his suffering and death on the cross had been out of obedience (Phil. 2:6ff). Just as Christ's death through obedience brings about his exaltation, so obedience is also required from every believer who is to be in eternal fellowship with God. That is why obedience to the Scriptures is so important, as we seek to reclaim authentic Anglicanism. We must not just preach the word, we must also obey it.

Third, in expounding the way of the cross in relation to his own suffering and death (24:27, 45-46), Christ makes it clear that a new dimension has been introduced to the eternal concept of the Davidic kingship predicted in 2 Samuel 7: this kingship could come only by way of the cross. As Jesus confronts his disciples with the reality of his presence here, he explains clearly to them God's final redemptive operation: that Christ is the restorer after the fall of man, whose blood was shed to effect a true exodus from a sin-infected life to a new life in Christ. This means that, by his death and resurrection, Christ has become the eternal exalted King from the line of David.

It is obvious that the usage of Old Testament passages by Jesus, here in Luke 24, as he talks with the disciples, shows that Scripture is continuous. It also

Just as Christ's death through obedience brings about his exaltation, so obedience is also required from every believer who is to be in eternal fellowship with God.

Study 4: The Son of God

shows that the entire Bible has the power to open human eyes to discover the mysteries of God (2 Timothy 3:16). In fact, by citing the Law of Moses. the Prophets and the Psalms, Christ affirms that all the Scriptures found their fulfilment in him. Indeed, in him all the promises of God are 'yes' and 'amen' (2 Corinthians 1:20).

Brethren, faithfulness rooted in obedience to Scripture is indeed the hallmark of authentic Anglicanism. It is through an in-depth study of the word that all obscurities surrounding our much cherished Anglican faith can be removed. The purpose of our gathering together at this conference is to develop genuine relationships with one another, as we study the word of God. We must do as Paul directs Timothy, 'Do your best to present yourself to God as one approved, a workman who does not need to be ashamed and who correctly handles the word of truth' (2 Timothy 2:15). Let us keep an open mind as we study the word of God, in which our faith is anchored. We are in the end time; we must remember that God will separate the wheat from the weeds (Matthew 13:30).

5. Luke 24:28-32

Having finished his teaching, Christ wanted to take leave of the two disciples (v28), but because by now his company has brought comfort and illumination to them, they desired that he stay with them. Then comes the breaking of the bread, an event which opened the eyes of the disciples! Nobody in genuine fellowship with Christ would want a cessation of such a fellowship. His companionship is physically and spiritually refreshing! What better place to reveal himself to the two disciples? The coming together of Christians around the Communion Table, with the pre-eminent place being given to the study of Scripture, should afford us the opportunity of seeing the awesome power of Christ more penetratingly. It was at the breaking of bread that the eyes of the disciples were opened. When

> *The coming together of Christians around the Communion Table, with the pre-eminent place being given to the study of Scripture, should afford us the opportunity of seeing the awesome power of Christ more penetratingly*

Study 4: The Son of God

Discussion Questions

Introductory question: What prevents people from accepting the idea of the resurrection of Jesus?

1. In this passage what place is given to the words of Jesus and to the Scriptures in the explaining of experience? How may we relate experience to Scripture?

2. What, according to Luke, is the relationship between encountering the risen Jesus, the Scriptures and a fellowship meal?

3. In this passage how is suffering evaluated in the light of glory?

we are gathered around the table, we should behold the beauty of the Lamb of God, who has been slain to reconcile us back to God. We should gather around the table in an attitude of total submission, asking Christ to show us what in our lives needs his divine touch. Are there some of us who are unfaithful in our marriage, proud and arrogant, or who have not been giving generously to support the work of God?

Beloved, it may be appropriate to ask, here, 'Why is God and his Christ hidden to our generation?' Many times we fail to see God because our eyes are closed to the truths of the Scriptures. Sometimes it is our fault, through neglect or liberal attitudes: we neglect the Scriptures in favour of worldly books, or we neglect the Holy Spirit (our Teacher) in favour of human wisdom. Sometimes, the problem is cultural conformity, because we do not allow Christ to replace this world at the centre of our souls (Romans 12:2).

6. Luke 24:49-53

In the closing verses of Luke 24, verses 49-53, we see the final charge of Jesus Christ to his disciples, to wait and be empowered in order to be able to bear witness to his resurrection power. For us, as we go home from here, many challenges will be waiting for us. But by the grace of God we shall prevail. As noted by the prophet Zechariah, the battle is the Lord's: '"Not by might nor by power, but by my Spirit," says the LORD Almighty' (Zechariah 4:6). Christ, having appeared to the disciples and eaten with them, commanded them to proclaim the good news of the Kingdom. They are to continue doing this until he comes back again, to reign in glory for ever and ever (Acts 1:11). Yes, we know that Jesus Christ is coming back as a glorious King at the end of the age. This is a sure hope, 'Everyone who has this hope in him purifies himself, just as he is pure' (1 John 3:3).

7. Conclusion

Beloved of God, as we await the coming of the King of kings, let us, in an attitude of obedience, continue to worship the risen Christ, acknowledging that we accept his Lordship over every area of our lives, as we return home to influence our generation as faithful Anglicans. The essence of this GAFCON Conference is to reaffirm our position, that we stand by the truth of Scripture. We are not here merely for a religious jamboree. We are here

---

4. *To what end is God leading his people, according to this passage?*

5. *What are the key themes, concerning the relationship between the risen Jesus and the Scriptures, that are highlighted in this teaching?*

6. *If Scripture is central to opening the eyes of unbelievers, so that they see who Jesus is, how should we share Scripture with those who have yet to believe?*

STUDY 4: THE SON OF GOD

as a body of Anglicans who are committed to the orthodoxy of the Scriptures. On this truth we stand, and shall always stand. Therefore, in the words of the prophet Isaiah, brethren, 'Arise, shine, for your light has come, and the glory of the LORD rises upon you' (Isaiah 60:1).

Bishop Michael Fape is Bishop of Remo, Nigeria. He received a B.A.(Hons) from the University of Ibadan, an S.T.M. from Yale University Divinity School, and a Ph.D from the University of Aberdeen. Before his election as Bishop in 2003, Dr Fape was the Dean of Archbishop Vining College of Theology in Akure, Nigeria. Among his published books are: Paul's Concept of Baptism (The Edwin Mellen Press, Lampeter, UK), and Knowing the Fundamentals of Anglicanism.
Bishop Fape is married to Toyin and they are blessed with three children.

Study 5: The Throne of God

Revelation 21
The Throne of God

Archbishop Datuk Yong Ping Chung

(Opening Prayer) O God our Father in Heaven, once again, before we open your words, we humbly bow down before your throne of grace, and we pray with joy and expectation that your Holy Spirit would open our hearts, minds and spirits to your living words. Help us to be totally teachable and receptive to the truth and blessing in your words. May your words bear fruit in our lives that we may glorify your Son, our Lord Jesus Christ. In Jesus' name we pray. Amen

Introduction

This is the last of the five Bible studies designed for GAFCON Jerusalem 2008. It is a joy and a privilege to share God's words with you on this final day of our conference. First, may I greet you all, using the greeting that the Apostle John sent to the seven churches in Asia Minor:

> Grace and peace to you from him who is, and who was, and who is to come, and from the seven spirits before

---

REVELATION 21

THE NEW JERUSALEM

¹Then I saw a new heaven and a new earth, for the first heaven and the first earth had passed away, and there was no longer any sea. ²I saw the Holy City, the new Jerusalem, coming down out of heaven from God, prepared as a bride beautifully dressed for her husband. ³And I heard a loud voice from the throne saying, "Now the dwelling of God is with men, and he will live with them. They will be his people, and God himself will be with them and be their God. ⁴He will wipe every tear from their eyes. There will be no more death or mourning or crying or pain, for the old order of things has passed away."
⁵He who was seated on the throne said, "I am making everything new!" Then he said, "Write this down, for these words are trustworthy and true."

⁶He said to me: "It is done. I am the Alpha and the Omega, the Beginning and the End. To him who is thirsty I will give to drink without cost from the spring of the water of life. ⁷He who overcomes will inherit all this, and I will be his God and he will be my son. ⁸But the cowardly, the unbelieving, the vile, the murderers, the sexually immoral, those who practice magic arts, the idolaters and all liars—their place will be in the fiery lake of burning sulphur. This is the second death."
⁹One of the seven angels who had the seven bowls full of the seven last plagues came and said to me, "Come, I will show you the bride, the wife of the

STUDY 5: THE THRONE OF GOD

Lamb." ¹⁰And he carried me away in the Spirit to a mountain great and high, and showed me the Holy City, Jerusalem, coming down out of heaven from God. ¹¹It shone with the glory of God, and its brilliance was like that of a very precious jewel, like a jasper, clear as crystal. ¹²It had a great, high wall with twelve gates, and with twelve angels at the gates. On the gates were written the names of the twelve tribes of Israel. ¹³There were three gates on the east, three on the north, three on the south and three on the west. ¹⁴The wall of the city had twelve foundations, and on them were the names of the twelve apostles of the Lamb.

¹⁵The angel who talked with me had a measuring rod of gold to measure the city, its gates and its walls. ¹⁶The city was laid out like a square, as long as it was wide. He measured the city with the rod and found it to be 12,000 stadia[a] in length, and as wide and high as it is long. ¹⁷He measured its wall and it was 144 cubits[b] thick,[c] by man's measurement, which the angel was using. ¹⁸The wall was made of jasper, and the city of pure gold, as pure as glass. ¹⁹The foundations of the city walls were decorated with every kind of precious stone. The first foundation was jasper, the second sapphire, the third chalcedony, the fourth emerald, ²⁰the fifth sardonyx, the sixth carnelian, the seventh chrysolite, the eighth beryl, the ninth topaz, the tenth chrysoprase, the eleventh jacinth, and the twelfth amethyst.[d] ²¹The twelve gates were twelve pearls, each gate made of a single pearl. The great street of the city was of

his throne, and from Jesus Christ, who is the faithful witness, the firstborn from the dead, and the ruler of the kings of the earth. (Revelation 1:4-5)

We have spent an amazing week together, as brothers and sisters in Christ and as fellow pilgrims. We have experienced, individually and together, as a community of faith, the reality of God's love and purpose, and we have been tracing the footsteps of our Lord and Saviour, Jesus Christ.

Our Bible expositors have ably led us into an understanding of the core of our existence: God created us and gave us a perfect place, Eden, where we could live in loving relationship with him and all that he had created, but we turned away from that, choosing our own way and allowing sin to enslave us. This has brought us nothing but fear, misery and eternal death. But our loving heavenly Father had a rescue plan for us, even from the beginning, to provide a way of restoring our relationship with him. He loved us so much that he was willing even to sacrifice his one and only Son, who would die for us so that we might live.

For God so loved the world that he gave his one and only Son, that whoever believes in him shall not perish but have eternal life. (John 3:16)

Jesus Christ, the Son of God, is our Saviour, our Lord and our King. He is our hope. He will lead us into a new, restored relationship with our God, and to the new Jerusalem, the perfect kingdom where he sits enthroned as our King for all eternity. He will rule with perfect love and with absolute authority.

How shall we understand this? Step by step our God brings us deeper into his Sanctuary, gradually revealing the depth of his love and commitment to us. He invites us into his throne room, to give us a glimpse of his glory and love. Today we will go to the last book of the Bible and enter, with the Apostle John, into the throne room of our God and Father. Let us see, with John, the glories of the heavenly court and hear what the Lord wants to say to us today. We will look at Revelation 21 and study this great chapter under three headings: the Context, the Throne, and the Future.

The context

Then I saw...(Revelation 21:1)

Who is this 'I' that saw? It is the author of the book of Revelation. The author identified

> *pure gold, like transparent glass. ²²I did not see a temple in the city, because the Lord God Almighty and the Lamb are its temple. ²³The city does not need the sun or the moon to shine on it, for the glory of God gives it light, and the Lamb is its lamp. ²⁴The nations will walk by its light, and the kings of the earth will bring their splendour into it. ²⁵On no day will its gates ever be shut, for there will be no night there. ²⁶The glory and honour of the nations will be brought into it. ²⁷Nothing impure will ever enter it, nor will anyone who does what is shameful or deceitful, but only those whose names are written in the Lamb's book of life.*
>
> *Footnotes:*
> a. Revelation 21:16 That is, about 1,400 miles (about 2,200 kilometers)
> b. Revelation 21:17 That is, about 200 feet (about 65 meters)
> c. Revelation 21:17 Or high
> d. Revelation 21:20 The precise identification of some of these precious stones is uncertain.

Study 5: The Throne of God

himself as 'his servant John' (1:1) or, simply, 'John' (1:4). From historical and internal evidences, scholars have worked out that the Apostle John wrote Revelation near the end of the reign of the Roman Emperor Domitian (AD 81-96). Domitian was the Emperor who demanded that all his subjects should worship him and address him as 'Lord and God'. This decree immediately created a head-on confrontation for the early Christians, who confessed and worshipped only Jesus as 'Lord and God', and refused to worship anyone else, the Emperor included. The book of Revelation contains many gruesome details of the sufferings and the killing of faithful believers who were unwilling to compromise. During this severe persecution ordered by Domitian, John, an elder of the early Christian community, was exiled on the island of Patmos, about fifty miles south-west of Ephesus, because he faithfully proclaimed the gospel of our Lord Jesus, remaining loyal and committed to him and to God's word (Revelation 1:9). Naturally, John was discouraged and at times he even despaired, because of this isolation from the main body of Christ, and also the constant fear and worry: enormous persecution and suffering were being put upon the tiny, fragile and powerless young church that he loved so much. Yet it was in just such a critical, desperate and turbulent time of suffering and persecution that the Lord of the Church took the initiative, and issued John with this command:

> 'Write on a scroll what you see and send it to the seven churches:' (Revelation 1:11)

and this invitation:

> 'Come up here, and I will show you what must take place after this.' (Revelation 4:1)

God knew what was going on. He was always in control. He took John up and gave him a series of visions. John was to take courage and stand firm. He was also to take action, and get on with the task of sharing the new vision from God with the people of God, in their experience of persecution and suffering. He had been given a message to pass on to the churches. Such is the love of our God, who bought his Church with the blood of his only begotten Son. Again and again he raises up his

Jesus Christ, the Son of God, is our Saviour, our Lord and our King. He is our hope.

Study 5: The Throne of God

servants to stand firm, and to defend and rescue his Church from the enemy's onslaught, which may be in the form of physical persecution, or else teaching that is erroneous, unfaithful and apostate.

You will have heard our Chairman outline for us, on the opening night, the crises of faith and leadership in our Communion in recent years. The attacks on our Communion have been likened to a spiritual genocide, a spiritual tsunami, or spiritual AIDS attacking our faith. At this very difficult time that we are going through, our living God has again taken a loving initiative, and issued an extraordinary invitation for us to be with him here in Jerusalem. From the very time we accepted our invitation to come here, we knew that we had responded to God's timely, urgent and clear call. We have gathered in Jerusalem humbly but boldly, cautiously but obediently, for GAFCON 2008. The whole of this last week has been time of celebration and spiritual feasting,

...He raises up his servants to stand firm, and to defend and rescue his Church from the enemy's on-slaught, which may be in the form of physical persecution, or else teaching that is erroneous, unfaithful and apostate

close to our Lord. Our inner spirits have soared high, and echoed the words of the psalmists:

> I rejoiced with those who said to me, 'Let us go to the house of the Lord.' Our feet are standing in your gates, O Jerusalem. (Psalm 122:1-2)

> Shout for joy to the Lord, all the earth. Worship the Lord with gladness; come before him with joyful songs. (Psalm 100:1-2)

> Enter his gates with thanksgiving and his courts with praise; give thanks to him and praise his name. For the Lord is good and his love endures forever; his faithfulness continues through all generations. (Psalm 100:4-5)

So, we are here. Representatives of the Anglican tribes totalling over 1200 precious souls, from 25 nations of the world, we have come to Jerusalem for GAFCON. This is the last day of our extra-ordinary, once-in-a-lifetime gathering. In worship, prayer, Bible studies, fellowship, and pilgrimage we have bowed down before the throne of our Lord, and

Study 5: The Throne of God

eagerly sought the face of the Lord. God has spoken to us. We have been blessed by our time together. Our hearts have been touched and our spirits stirred, both as individuals and as a conference. We experienced unity in spirit and in truth. Deep in our souls we have had a special encounter with our living God. We have shared the experience of the two disciples who met the risen Christ on the road to Emmaus:

> Were not our hearts burning within us while he talked with us on the road and opened the Scriptures to us? (Luke 24:32)

We all know that GAFCON, in Jerusalem 2008, cannot have been and is not a dreamt-up human strategy, or a calculated response of the flesh, designed to produce a competitive, worldly solution in answer to the crises of faith and leadership in our time. God has brought us to the Holy Land, the land in which he chose to lay out his 'story of salvation' after the Creation. Our Bible studies have retraced that same eternal agenda which is closest to his heart. He wants to imprint his words on our hearts, and knit our hearts together as we build on the rock foundation of his words. Then we shall be connected to his own heart's desire, which is to map out a rescue plan for the Anglican Communion we love. This is God's doing. GAFCON is about God and not about us.

I am very sure that God does not want us to be here just to redesign the 'box', to tinker with the existing culture in the Communion. This has failed us miserably, enslaving our Communion, corrupting some of our top leaders, blunting the cutting edge of the Gospel, and sidetracking our Communion from its mission agenda for such a long time. We would have missed the whole point, and paid too much, if we continued to fix our eyes on the human stage, playing a human game with only the values of the human heart. It is time for us to wake up and admit that our Communion is very sick. It is critically important, also, that we realize what has been going on: a massive death trap has been designed by some in our Communion, with the clear intention of eroding and changing the fundamentals of the Gospel. This process has been

God does not want us to be here just to redesign the 'box', to tinker with the existing culture in the Communion.

Study 5: The Throne of God

devised and implemented in such a way that it will continue indefinitely, until it has quite sapped our energy and achieved the desired result, that of dulling the conscience of our whole Communion, so that we will accommodate the biggest compromise of all time, and ...

... walk in the counsel of the wicked

... stand in the way of sinners

... sit in the seat of mockers (Psalm 1:1)

For many years now 'a gallows seventy-five feet high', to borrow an image from the book of Esther, has been skilfully and determinedly constructed and put in place for the sole purpose of hanging the Biblical, Christ-centred and spirit-filled orthodox and evangelical witnesses in the Anglican Communion. GAFCON 2008 is the trumpet call for us to heed Mordecai's warning:

> 'Do not think that because you are in the king's house you alone of all the Jews will escape. For if you remain silent at this time, relief and deliverance for the Jews will arise from another place, but you and your father's family will perish. And who knows but that you have come to royal position for such a time as this?' (Esther 4:13-14)

God spoke in the day of Esther and in the day of John, as the Bible has recorded for us. God continues to speak to us in our day through his own words. The experience of the last few days has sharpened our focus and also, importantly, our understanding of our *context*, in both the temporal and the spiritual realm. We must learn our lesson and take seriously the warning from the Bible. God has invited us here to Jerusalem to give us his own vision, and issue anew his challenges to us for such a time as this.

In our context today we must only say what the Lord has given us to say, no more and no less

Our friends in different parts of the world have been deep in prayer. They are waiting for us to share with them the message of hope from God himself. The world is watching and waiting too. But many may have already made up their minds about what they expect us to say. In our context today we must only say what the Lord has given us to say, no more and no less.

Study 5: The Throne of God

The throne

And I heard a loud voice from the throne ... (Revelation 21:3)

Like many of us, John needed a visual aid, and God, in his loving kindness and generous wisdom, provided it for him. From the very beginning of the book of Revelation, John was given clear and precise pictures (Revelation 1:12-20). In chapter 4 there is even an open door in heaven for John to walk through. Immediately after the invitation:

> 'Come up here, and I will show you what must take place after this' (Revelation 4:1b)

John records:

> At once I was in the Spirit, and there before me was a throne in heaven with someone sitting on it. (Revelation 4:2)

Then the whole of Revelation 4 goes on to describe the throne room, in elaborate and glorious detail, and also the worship in the heavenly court. The throne in Revelation 21:3 is the same as that in Revelation 4. It is the throne of God, and God alone. It is the throne of the perfect King, promised by God for his people. The fulfilment of that very special promise of God is this ultimate King, who sits on the throne of dominion, power, authority and glory. He is that perfect King, chosen and appointed by God from the line of David, whose reign will have the favour and blessing of God for ever and ever. Yet, by God's own doing, it is also the throne of the lamb who was slain. For John, this is the throne of the ascended Christ, the King of Glory. He and he alone is worthy

> '... to receive power and wealth and wisdom and strength and honour and glory and praise!'
> (Revelation 5:12)

From this glorious and unique throne of grace come amazing words of authority and power. John needed to hear them all – praise God that he was there to receive them! For our part, we are deeply grateful that God has gathered us here in Jerusalem, to hear and receive his special words for us at this critical moment for our Communion. Let us hear the three 'words' coming from that eternal throne.

> *Like many of us, John needed a visual aid, and God, in His loving kindness and generous wisdom, provided it for him*

Study 5: The Throne of God

1. *'I am the Alpha and Omega, the Beginning and the End (Revelation 21:6)*

These are words from him 'who was seated on the throne'. He is the absolute Alpha. He is the first, the beginning. Before him there was nothing. There was no 'before him'. And he is the absolute Omega. He is the last, the end. Nothing comes after him. He is eternal. There is no 'after him'. All life flows *from* him, and all life flows *back* to him. 'For in him we live and move and have our being.' (Acts 17:28) He is the ascended Christ and the King of Glory. This is our God, who has invited us here to lay aside all our own desires, ambitions, likes and dislikes, and our agendas. Yes, this means that all our crowns must be laid before the throne in order to honour, glorify and magnify his name. GAFCON will have no future if we continue to long for what a human king can give us, and fashion our ministry and work to please an earthly king. Brothers and sisters in Christ, all of us are leaders in our church. God has called us to lay our crowns before the throne today.

God has called us to lay our crowns before the throne today

2. *'I am making everything new!' (Revelation 21:5)*

The heart's desire of God the Father is to create us for his own glory (Genesis 1:27, Ephesians 1:4-6), and to redeem us when we fall (1 Peter 1:18-20). He promises to give us a new heart (Ezekiel 36:26). Jesus understood the heart of his Father and commanded that we should be born again (John 3:3, 5). Paul, after his own experience of being born again, was able to grasp the truth and the vital importance of new life in Jesus, and so he declared, uncompromisingly:

> Therefore, if anyone is in Christ, he is a new creation; the old has gone, the new has come! (2 Corinthians 5:17)

Jesus the King, who sits on the throne, longs that each one of us should have that experience of being born again in him. And he longs that his people should catch the Pentecostal fire, and go and win lost souls for him. He also desires that his Church should make disciples who, in turn, will go and make more disciples (2 Timothy 2:2).

'I am making everything new!' is the heart's desire of our

Study 5: The Throne of God

Lord, Saviour and King. He has invited us to come to this gathering to remind us that he requires us to be new beings, as individual leaders, as a collection of provinces, and as the bold witnesses of the Christ-centred, Spirit-filled, Biblical, orthodox and evangelical movement in our Communion and our world today. No human effort can make new our sick Communion. But the Holy Spirit can and will. This renewing work of God, however, must begin with us.

> *The heart's desire of God the Father is to create us for his own glory, and to redeem us when we fall*

6:23), but the Resurrection of Christ Jesus is the final blow from God that defeats death. Henceforth, death has no more power over the promised King who bore our sin. Now the word of the Cross is the power of salvation, leading to repentance and the forgiveness of sins. New life in Christ, by the Holy Spirit, can now be a reality. I am sure that each of us in this conference will have our own personal story to tell, of this finished work of Christ in us. Praise the Lord!

3. 'It is done.' (Revelation 21:6)

This is the testimony of the lamb who was slain on the Cross. It also echoes what Jesus, our Lord and Saviour, declared on the Cross: 'It is finished.' (John 19:30) Yes, Jesus has fulfilled the requirements of the Law and Prophets. He has fulfilled the Law of Sacrifice as the Lamb of God. His blood has been shed for the forgiveness of sins. The mission he had been sent to do has been accomplished, and God has given it the seal of his approval by rolling away the stone on the day of the Resurrection. The wages of sin is death (Roman

The future

Then I saw a new heaven and a new earth ... (Revelation 21:1)

I saw the Holy City, the new Jerusalem ... (Revelation 21:2)

The words that John heard were words of truth, with power and authority. But what he saw was equally awesome and glorious. He saw a new heaven and a new earth. This new heaven and new earth was made clear by the New Jerusalem.

John, being a Jew, understood the deep significance of Jerusalem for the God's people in the Old Testament. He knew

Study 5: The Throne of God

from the Old Testament that Jerusalem was the city where God had chosen 'to put his Name' (Deuteronomy 12:5,11,21). Jerusalem was the city where the temple of the living God was to be built. Hence this was the 'Holy City', 'the City of God', 'the City of the Lord'. All male Israelites were ordered to travel to Jerusalem three times a year.

In Jerusalem God revealed his word to his people (Isaiah 2:3), and from there he ruled over them (Psalm 99:1-2). When the Israelites prayed they were to face this Holy City. God had also made a promise to them:

> As the mountains surround Jerusalem, so the Lord surrounds his people both now and forevermore. (Psalm 125:2)

Indeed, Jerusalem was a symbol of what God required of his people in the Old Testament. When God's people came to Jerusalem they would be reminded of God's sovereign power, his holiness and his faithfulness. But most important of all, they would remember his eternal commitment to be their God.

These things are all good and wonderful, but when God broke in and gave John the vision of Jerusalem, he allowed him to see the new Jerusalem. This new Jerusalem is no longer an earthly city but a heavenly city (Galatians.4:26), where God dwells and Christ rules at his right hand. God has set this up for his own glory. When we come to Christ, we 'have come to Mount Zion, to the heavenly Jerusalem, the city of the living God' (Hebrews 12:22).

John saw this new Jerusalem 'coming down out of heaven from God, prepared as a bride beautifully dressed for her husband' (Revelation 21:2). He heard a loud voice from the throne, declaring:

> 'Now the dwelling of God is with men, and he will live with them. They will be his people, and God himself will be with them and be their God. He will wipe every tear from their eyes. There will be no more death or

this was the day God had foretold: God's covenant promises had been fulfilled, sin had been defeated, and the effects of sin, such as sorrow, pain, unhappiness and death, had been banished forever.

Study 5: The Throne of God

Discussion Questions

Introductory question: What happens in our lives or the lives of others when hope for the future is lost?

1. Martin Luther King said, 'I have a dream.' What is the role of a vision of the future in people's lives?

2. What, according to the passage, is God's purpose for the future of humanity and for the whole created order?

3. What are the key themes, concerning what God is creating as his new future, that are highlighted in this teaching?

mourning or crying or pain, for the old order of things has passed away.'
(Revelation 21:3-4)

John realized that this was the day God had foretold: God's covenant promises had been fulfilled, sin had been defeated, and the effects of sin, such as sorrow, pain, unhappiness and death, had been banished forever.

More extraordinary than this, John testified:

> I did not see a temple in the city because the Lord God Almighty and the Lamb are its temple. The city does not need the sun or the moon to shine on it, for the glory of God gives it light, and the Lamb is its lamp.
> (Revelation 21:22-23)

God invited John to be with him and gave him the visions in Revelation, so that he could stand firm and get on with the mission God had given him. He was to challenge those early Christians to share the Gospel of the Lord Jesus among all nations, making disciples all over the world, so that:

> The nations will walk by its light, and the kings of the earth will bring their splendour into it.
> (Revelation 21:24)

STUDY 5: THE THRONE OF GOD

We have come to Jerusalem, this week, to seek God's face. Indeed, our life together and our visits to the various sites have helped us to link up with one another, and with the history of our faith in Jesus Christ; we have been given inspiration and sustenance to do the work we were called to do. There was great rejoicing, and much thanksgiving, when the draft of the Statement on the Global Anglican Future was presented to our assembly at noon on Friday. Later this morning we will adopt the official statement. We have rejoiced that a strong, clear, gracious, wise and bold Statement has been drafted. I believe God's vision for us at this time is very clear to all who have attended this Global Anglican Future Conference. We will leave this earthly Jerusalem with the vision of God's new Jerusalem. In this GAFCON 2008, God has challenged and commissioned us to be BRAVE and BOLD leaders in our churches and in our Communion.

BRAVE stands for Biblical, Relevant, Action, Visionary and Evangelistic, and BOLD stands for Biblical, Obedient, Loving and Dynamic!

Concluding challenge

Brothers and sisters in Christ,

4. What, according to this passage and exposition, is God creating anew, and what does this mean for the church now?

5. What has the finished work of Christ accomplished, and what does this mean, now, for our struggle with the debilitating powers of sin and death?

6. What does our knowledge of the old Jerusalem tell us about the experience of the new Jerusalem?

7. How is the vision of the new Jerusalem to inform our lives now?

Study 5: The Throne of God

after GAFCON 2008 our life and ministry will never be the same again. Let us go back to our churches and be God's servants who are Biblical, Relevant, Action-minded, Visionary, Evangelistic, Obedient, Loving and Dynamic. Our churches need BOLD & BRAVE leaders. Our Communion needs BOLD & BRAVE leaders – the Anglican Communion can *only* be saved by BOLD & BRAVE leaders.

May God bless you all.

Archbishop Datuk Yong Ping Chung retired as Bishop of Sabah in Malaysia and Primate of South East Asia in 2005. He is married to Julia, and has two daughters and two grandchildren. He was Chairman of the Anglican Consultative Council from 1984-1990. He has consistently given encouragement to faithful orthodox Anglicans in North America, and provided them with fellowship and support. He has been honoured by the Government of Malaysia with their highest honour as Datuk.

Jude
The Authority of God

Bishop Wallace Benn

We all know how wonderful, powerful and relevant the Bible is, as 'God's word written'. But recently I have rediscovered the Epistle of Jude and been amazed at how relevant it is, and how powerfully it speaks into the current situation in the Anglican Communion. One commentator puts it well: 'The epistle of Jude is an impassioned exhortation to a church that finds itself living in the midst of ethical lapse and doctrinal compromise.' (*Expositor's Bible Commentary* (revised) on *Jude*)

Introduction

Jude was probably the brother of James, the leader of the Jerusalem church. Both were half-brothers of the Lord Jesus. But in his opening words it is not earthly privilege or human ancestry that Jude appeals to, but rather the privilege of being a servant of Jesus Christ. The Son of God had become a servant, becoming 'obedient to death', and Jude saw that the greatest self-designation was as a servant of this Jesus.

JUDE

¹*Jude, a servant of Jesus Christ and a brother of James,*

To those who have been called, who are loved by God the Father and kept by [a] *Jesus Christ:*

²*Mercy, peace and love be yours in abundance.*

THE SIN AND DOOM OF GODLESS MEN
³*Dear friends, although I was very eager to write to you about the salvation we share, I felt I had to write and urge you to contend for the faith that was once for all entrusted to the saints.* ⁴*For certain men whose condemnation was written about*[b] *long ago have secretly slipped in among you. They are godless men, who change the grace of our God into a license for immorality and deny Jesus Christ our only Sovereign and Lord.*

⁵*Though you already know all this, I want to remind you that the Lord*[c] *delivered his people out of Egypt, but later destroyed those who did not believe.* ⁶*And the angels who did not keep their positions of authority but abandoned their own home—these he has kept in darkness, bound with everlasting chains for judgment on the great Day.* ⁷*In a similar way, Sodom and Gomorrah and the surrounding towns gave themselves up to sexual immorality and perversion. They serve as an example of those who suffer the punishment of eternal fire.*

⁸*In the very same way, these dreamers pollute their own bodies, reject authority and slander celestial beings.* ⁹*But even the archangel Michael, when he was disputing with the devil about the body*

Study 6: The Authority of God

of Moses, did not dare to bring a slanderous accusation against him, but said, "The Lord rebuke you!" ¹⁰Yet these men speak abusively against whatever they do not understand; and what things they do understand by instinct, like unreasoning animals—these are the very things that destroy them.

¹¹Woe to them! They have taken the way of Cain; they have rushed for profit into Balaam's error; they have been destroyed in Korah's rebellion.

¹²These men are blemishes at your love feasts, eating with you without the slightest qualm—shepherds who feed only themselves. They are clouds without rain, blown along by the wind; autumn trees, without fruit and uprooted—twice dead. ¹³They are wild waves of the sea, foaming up their shame; wandering stars, for whom blackest darkness has been reserved forever.

¹⁴Enoch, the seventh from Adam, prophesied about these men: "See, the Lord is coming with thousands upon thousands of his holy ones ¹⁵to judge everyone, and to convict all the ungodly of all the ungodly acts they have done in the ungodly way, and of all the harsh words ungodly sinners have spoken against him." ¹⁶These men are grumblers and faultfinders; they follow their own evil desires; they boast about themselves and flatter

Jude and James were both reluctant to become believers, but it appears that they did so after the crucifixion and resurrection of their half-brother, Jesus.

The letter is addressed to 'those who have been called, who are loved by God the Father and kept by Jesus Christ' (v1b). This threefold description of what it means to be a Christian is powerful and delightful. 'Called' means effectually called, i.e. called and energised to respond. Those who are called in this way, and who respond to the Gospel, are beloved by God. Further, they are kept, literally, 'by' or 'for' Jesus Christ – both meanings are gloriously true! In the greeting Jude replaces the Pauline word 'grace' with 'mercy' (v2), which means the same thing except that it emphasises a little more, perhaps, the undeserved nature of God's love towards us.

2. The main point (vv2,3)

Jude tells us his reason for writing. He had hoped to write them a letter about 'the salvation we share' (v2), but because of the danger the church is facing – false teaching has been leading to Christ-denying living – he feels obliged to write to them in order to 'contend for the faith that was once for all entrusted to the saints' (v3). It is important to recognise where Jude's heart is: he would much rather have written about the grace of God in the

Study 6: The Authority of God

salvation that true Christians enjoy, but he knew it was necessary to fight for, and to defend, Apostolic truth. Which of us today, like Jude, would not love to be able to speak about the Gospel directly, without having to address the issues of immorality, homosexual practice etc., which have caused our Communion so much trouble! But if we are to be faithful to our Lord we must address the presenting issues of our day, issues that threaten the Church's health and wellbeing. These issues could cause us to draw away from Apostolic teaching and life, and so from the Gospel of our Saviour.

The Greek word for 'contend' is a strengthened form of the word 'to agonise'. Here Jude employs an athletic metaphor taken from the gymnasium. The image calls to mind a wrestling match. For believers, the implication is that they are involved in an intense moral struggle over truth.

> 'The struggle Jude has in mind is the presentation of the received faith over against the theological/moral novelty of the heretics (v3b-4), the growth in that faith and the avoidance of error (v20-21), and the rescue of those who have been drawn into the errorists' snare (v22-23). Jude's call pertains to both the doctrinal and moral issues raised by the heretics'

(Gene L. Green, *Baker Exegetical Commentary on the New Testament: Jude and 2 Peter*, page 56).

---

others for their own advantage.

A CALL TO PERSEVERE
[17]But, dear friends, remember what the apostles of our Lord Jesus Christ foretold. [18]They said to you, "In the last times there will be scoffers who will follow their own ungodly desires." [19]These are the men who divide you, who follow mere natural instincts and do not have the Spirit.

[20]But you, dear friends, build yourselves up in your most holy faith and pray in the Holy Spirit. [21]Keep yourselves in God's love as you wait for the mercy of our Lord Jesus Christ to bring you to eternal life.

[22]Be merciful to those who doubt; [23]snatch others from the fire and save them; to others show mercy, mixed with fear—hating even the clothing stained by corrupted flesh.

DOXOLOGY
[24]To him who is able to keep you from falling and to present you before his glorious presence without fault and with great joy— [25]to the only God our Saviour be glory, majesty, power and authority, through Jesus Christ our Lord, before all ages, now and forevermore! Amen.

Footnotes:
a. Jude 1:1 Or *for*, or *in*
b. Jude 1:4 Or *men who were marked out for condemnation*
c. Jude 1:5 Some early manuscripts *Jesus*

Study 6: The Authority of God

Note that the faith is 'once for all entrusted' – it is revealed by God, and it is not to be altered or tampered with. Each generation of new believers is based on the same Apostolic foundation, which we find in the pages of the New Testament. We are called to be faithful to that.

3. The identification of those causing problems (v4)

1. *The false teachers 'have secretly slipped in among you' (v4a)*

The words implies stealth, as if the false teachers were spies, but they also remind us that these people 'appeared' to be real believers. Here the danger for the church appears to be from within!

2. *They pervert the grace of God into 'a licence for immorality' (v4)*

They teach that the Gospel sets us free to be ourselves, rather than saving us by grace so that we may become holy, and be conformed to the image of God's Son.

3. *The lifestyle they advocate denies the Lord Jesus (v4c)*

It is not just false doctrine that denies the Lordship of Christ; false living also denies his Lordship!

> *It is not just false doctrine that denies the Lordship of Christ; false living also denies his Lordship! Orthodoxy and orthopraxy are equally important.*

Orthodoxy and orthopraxy are equally important.

4. The characteristics of the false teaching and practice (vv5-11)

Jude now sets out the characteristics of the false teaching and practice he has seen. (From our own experience we might add that proponents of false teaching and practice will usually claim that Jude's evaluation is not true!)

The false teaching (and practice) is really:

- a crisis of belief (v5)
- a denial of legitimate authority in the church (v6, v8)
- a denial of the Bible's standard on sexual morality

On this last point, the Bible teaches that the God-given context for sexual intimacy is between one man and one woman in heterosexual marriage. Anything outside that, either heterosexually or homosexually, is not God's will for us (and our Maker knows best!). Homosexual practice is clearly included, in v7, in the reference to Sodom and

Study 6: The Authority of God

Gomorrah, and the pursuing of what, from God's point of view, is 'perversion' (or 'unnatural desire' ESV).

The heart of the problem with the false teachers is that, by rejecting Apostolic authority, they are in fact rejecting God's authority. They do this because they exalt the authority of their own experience ('these dreamers' v 8) over and above God's authority, and they argue ('like unreasoning animals' v10) that following your own instincts is the right way to go. 'If it feels right,' they say, 'it is right!' (v18). But Jude says, 'Woe to them!' (v11).

Cain, Balaam and Korah are used as examples of ungodliness, selfish profit and insubordination. (Check out their stories – in Genesis 4:2b-16, Numbers 22-24 and Numbers 16 – and avoid following their examples!)

5. Wonderful pictures and Jude's assessment (vv12-16)

1. These false teachers are 'blemishes at your love feast' (v12a). Literally, they are like 'reefs' which cause spiritual shipwreck! They share 'communion' but actually they are out of communion.

2. They are like 'clouds without rain' (v12b). They promise much – e.g. credibility with the contemporary world, and the growth of the church once it is more in tune with current values – but they deliver little or nothing.

3. They are like 'autumn trees, without fruit and uprooted' (v12c) – they don't deliver a spiritual harvest.

4. They are like 'wild waves of the sea' (v13a) – they make plenty of noise and fuss but they have no boundaries.

5. They are like 'wandering stars' (v13b) – they have no constraint, and they cannot keep you on course spiritually.

They are also grumblers and fault-finders who follow their own sinful desires, seeking to cover these with a veil of religiosity (v16).

All this is critically important, says Jude. Judgement does await those who persist in disobeying God's will and his word (vv14,15).

What is the solution for God's people who want to follow their Lord and obey his Word? The solution is 'to contend for the faith'. But how exactly is that to be done?

STUDY 6: THE AUTHORITY OF GOD

Discussion Questions

Introductory question: Why are many Christians surprised when there is conflict in the church?

1. Vinay Samuel writes in the Introduction, 'The Way of the Cross exposes the true nature of the evil one's propaganda, and enables the disciple to address the real world.' How does the book of Jude confirm this insight?

2. Compare Jude's description of the servants of God with his description of their opponents.

3. How do the five analogies in verses 12 and 13 help us to understand the false ideas that threaten the church's life?

6. Jude's condemnation of false teaching and practice (vv17-19)

Jude has already shown us the enormous seriousness of the problem – eternity is at stake (v7)! False teaching and false practice make a first-order danger for the Church, a Gospel-denying and Christ-denying danger. It is false teaching and false living that cause divisions in the Church, not those Christians who seek to be faithful to Apostolic teaching and practice (v19)!

7. By contrast ... (vv20-23)

'But you, dear friends ...' (v20)

Having analysed and addressed the problem, what is the solution for God's people who want to follow their Lord and obey his Word? The solution is 'to contend for the faith' (v3). But how exactly is that to be done? Jude uses four verbs (in vv20,21):

I. **'Build** *yourselves up in your most holy faith'* This side of heaven we live on a building site! We are to build ourselves up, by reading the Bible and listening to it being taught, and praying home its teaching in our lives, with the support of other believers seeking to so the same.

Our faith is holy – therefore it has boundaries!

Our faith is holy – it calls us to holiness of life!

Literally, the verse means 'Build yourself *upon* your most holy faith'. The Gospel and the word of God are the only foundation of a believer's life of obedience and holiness.

2. **'Pray** in the Holy Spirit' Prayer is the weapon of our warfare! As we depend upon God, he will help us, strengthen us, and equip us for daily living. Prayer is also the means of moving mountainous problems!

3. **'Keep** yourselves in God's love' This is the key imperative among the four verbs (the others are participles). It is *so* important. All our efforts in serving the Lord need to come from a love relationship with the Lord; otherwise, devotion to the one who 'loved me and gave himself for me' (Galatians 2:20) will become grudging duty. As a friend put it to me, 'A Christian cannot live safely more than six inches away from the foot of the Cross!'

4. **'Wait** for the mercy of our Lord Jesus Christ' We wait for the consummation of all that Jesus has won for us. So we are *future* people, who need to learn to wait patiently for God's purposes to be fulfilled.

These are the four key verbs

STUDY 6: THE AUTHORITY OF GOD

4. What are the key themes, concerning the source of the problems in the church, and the best ways to respond to them, that are highlighted in this teaching?

5. How, according to this passage and exposition, can we discern whether people are rejecting the authority of God?

6. How are we to express the authority of God in our lives, as we embrace the Way of the Cross?

7. How may we help others to recognize and obey the authority of God?

which will keep us on course spiritually, but we have *practical* duties too:

(a) *'Be merciful to those who doubt'* (v22), and show mercy generally in our dealings with people, without dropping God's standards.

(b) *'Snatch others from the fire and save them'* (v23). If we love people we will want to see them come to know Jesus as Saviour and Lord, and prayerfully, lovingly and sensitively we will seek to win them for him.

8. Joyful conclusion (vv24,25)

As we can now see, Jude is far from advocating a sort of Pharisaical, unloving hard line. No, while he does call for courageous, unswerving loyalty to Jesus, and therefore to the Apostolic deposit of faith, this call is combined with an evangelist's love for people, and a longing to see them won for our Saviour.

And who is sufficient for these things! Certainly we cannot cope on our own. But our confidence is in the God who loves us, and in whose grace and mercy we stand because of Jesus. He will see us through.

So the epistle ends with a great doxology to God's determined love for his people. He will keep us from falling – 'keep' is one of the great words in *Jude*, it is mentioned six times; and 'falling', or 'stumbling' is, literally, the uncertain faltering of a horse on slippery ground. But our God will keep us through all the hard, difficult and dangerous times, and bring us joyfully into his presence in heaven one day. In the meantime, he can be trusted never to give up on us!

That should fill us with joy!

Study 6: The Authority of God

The Right Reverend Wallace Benn has been Area Bishop of Lewes since 1997. He lives with his wife Lindsay in Eastbourne, East Sussex, and they have a married daughter and a son at university. As well as being an experienced parish clergyman, having spent twenty-five years in parochial ministry, he is a well-known inspirational teacher and speaker, and a published author who has also written articles in various theological journals. He is particularly keen to see the Word of God honoured and believed. Wallace is President of the Church of England Evangelical Council and Chairman of Bible by the Beach, a new yearly Bible teaching initiative in Eastbourne. He is an enthusiastic rugby watcher and supporter, and enjoys motor racing.

Statement on the Global Anglican Future

> Praise the LORD!
>
> It is good to sing praises to our God; for he is gracious, and a song of praise is fitting.
>
> The LORD builds up Jerusalem; he gathers the outcasts of Israel. (Psalm 147:1-2)

Brothers and Sisters in Christ: We, the participants in the Global Anglican Future Conference, send you greetings from Jerusalem!

Introduction

The Global Anglican Future Conference (GAFCON), which was held in Jerusalem from 22-29 June 2008, is a spiritual movement to preserve and promote the truth and power of the gospel of salvation in Jesus Christ as we Anglicans have received it. The movement is *global*: it has mobilised Anglicans from around the world. We are *Anglican*: 1148 lay and clergy participants, including 291 bishops representing millions of faithful Anglican Christians. We cherish our Anglican heritage and the Anglican Communion and have no intention of departing from it. And we believe that, in God's providence, Anglicanism has a *bright future* in obedience to our Lord's Great Commission to make disciples of all nations and to build up the church on the foundation of biblical truth (Matthew 28:18-20; Ephesians 2:20).

GAFCON is not just a moment in time, but a movement in the Spirit, and we hereby:

- launch the GAFCON movement as a fellowship of confessing Anglicans
- publish the Jerusalem Declaration as the basis of the fellowship
- encourage GAFCON Primates to form a Council.

The Global Anglican Context

The future of the Anglican Communion is but a piece of the wider scenario of opportunities and challenges for the gospel in 21st century global culture. We rejoice in the way God has opened doors for gospel mission among many peoples, but we grieve for the spiritual decline in the most economically developed nations, where the forces of militant secularism and pluralism are eating away the fabric of society and churches are compromised and enfeebled in their witness. The vacuum left by them is readily filled by other faiths and deceptive cults. To meet these challenges will require Christians to work together to understand and oppose these forces and to liberate those under their sway. It will entail the planting of new churches among unreached peoples and also committed action to restore authentic Christianity to compromised churches.

The Anglican Communion, present in six continents, is well positioned to address this challenge, but currently it is divided and distracted. The Global Anglican Future Conference merged in response to a crisis within the Anglican Communion, a crisis involving *three undeniable facts* concerning world Anglicanism.

The first fact is the acceptance and promotion within the provinces of the Anglican Communion of a different 'gospel' (cf. Galatians 1:6-8) which is contrary to the apostolic gospel. This false gospel undermines the authority of God's Word written and the uniqueness of Jesus Christ as the author of salvation from sin, death and judgement. Many of its proponents claim that all religions offer equal access to God and that Jesus is only a way, not the way, the truth and the life. It promotes a variety of sexual preferences and immoral behaviour as a universal human right. It claims God's blessing for same-sex unions over against the biblical teaching on holy matrimony. In 2003 this false gospel led to the consecration of a bishop living in a homosexual relationship.

The second fact is the declaration by provincial bodies in the Global South that they are out of communion with bishops and churches that promote this false gospel. These declarations have resulted in a realignment whereby faithful Anglican Christians have left existing territorial parishes, dioceses and provinces in certain Western churches and become members of other dioceses and provinces, all within the Anglican Communion. These actions have also led to the appointment of new Anglican bishops set over geographic areas already occupied by other Anglican bishops. A major realignment has occurred and will continue to unfold.

The third fact is the manifest failure of the Communion Instruments to exercise discipline in the face of overt heterodoxy. The Episcopal Church USA and the Anglican Church of Canada, in proclaiming this false gospel, have consistently defied the 1998 Lambeth statement of biblical moral principle (Resolution 1.10). Despite numerous meetings and reports to and from the

'Instruments of Unity,' no effective action has been taken, and the bishops of these unrepentant churches are welcomed to Lambeth 2008. To make matters worse, there has been a failure to honour promises of discipline, the authority of the Primates' Meeting has been undermined and the Lambeth Conference has been structured so as to avoid any hard decisions. We can only come to the devastating conclusion that 'we are a global Communion with a colonial structure'.

Sadly, this crisis has torn the fabric of the Communion in such a way that it cannot simply be patched back together. At the same time, it has brought together many Anglicans across the globe into personal and pastoral relationships in a fellowship which is faithful to biblical teaching, more representative of the demographic distribution of global Anglicanism today and stronger as an instrument of effective mission, ministry and social involvement.

A Fellowship of Confessing Anglicans

We, the participants in the Global Anglican Future Conference, are a fellowship of confessing Anglicans for the benefit of the Church and the furtherance of its mission. We are a *fellowship* of people united in the communion (*koinonia*) of the one Spirit and committed to work and pray together in the common mission of Christ. It is a *confessing* fellowship in that its members confess the faith of Christ crucified, stand firm for the gospel in the global and Anglican context, and affirm a contemporary rule, the Jerusalem Declaration, to guide the movement for the future. We are a fellowship of *Anglicans*, including provinces, dioceses, churches, missionary jurisdictions, para-church organisations and individual Anglican Christians whose goal is to reform, heal and revitalise the Anglican Communion and expand its mission to the world.

Our fellowship is not breaking away from the Anglican Communion. We, together with many other faithful Anglicans throughout the world, believe the doctrinal foundation of Anglicanism, which defines our core identity as Anglicans, is expressed in these words:

> The doctrine of the Church is grounded in the Holy Scriptures and in such teachings of the ancient Fathers and Councils of the Church as are

agreeable to the said Scriptures. In particular, such doctrine is to be found in the Thirty-nine Articles of Religion, the Book of Common Prayer and the Ordinal.

We intend to remain faithful to this standard, and we call on others in the Communion to reaffirm and return to it. While acknowledging the nature of Canterbury as an historic see, we do not accept that Anglican identity is determined necessarily through recognition by the Archbishop of Canterbury. Building on the above doctrinal foundation of Anglican identity, we hereby publish the Jerusalem Declaration as the basis of our fellowship.

The Jerusalem Declaration

In the name of God the Father, God the Son and God the Holy Spirit:

We, the participants in the Global Anglican Future Conference, have met in the land of Jesus' birth. We express our loyalty as disciples to the King of kings, the Lord Jesus. We joyfully embrace his command to proclaim the reality of his kingdom which he first announced in this land. The gospel of the kingdom is the good news of salvation, liberation and transformation for all. In light of the above, we agree to chart a way forward together that promotes and protects the biblical gospel and mission to the world, solemnly declaring the following tenets of orthodoxy which underpin our Anglican identity.

We rejoice in the gospel of God through which we have been saved by grace through faith in Jesus Christ by the power of the Holy Spirit. Because God first loved us, we love him and as believers bring forth fruits of love, ongoing repentance, lively hope and thanksgiving to God in all things.

We believe the Holy Scriptures of the Old and New Testaments to be the Word of God written and to contain all things necessary for salvation. The Bible is to be translated, read, preached, taught and obeyed in its plain and canonical sense, respectful of the church's historic and consensual reading.

We uphold the four Ecumenical Councils and the three historic Creeds as expressing the rule of faith of the one holy catholic and apostolic Church.

We uphold the Thirty-nine Articles as containing the true

doctrine of the Church agreeing with God's Word and as authoritative for Anglicans today.

We gladly proclaim and submit to the unique and universal Lordship of Jesus Christ, the Son of God, humanity's only Saviour from sin, judgement and hell, who lived the life we could not live and died the death that we deserve. By his atoning death and glorious resurrection, he secured the redemption of all who come to him in repentance and faith.

We rejoice in our Anglican sacramental and liturgical heritage as an expression of the gospel, and we uphold the 1662 Book of Common Prayer as a true and authoritative standard of worship and prayer, to be translated and locally adapted for each culture.

We recognise that God has called and gifted bishops, priests and deacons in historic succession to equip all the people of God for their ministry in the world. We uphold the classic Anglican Ordinal as an authoritative standard of clerical orders.

We acknowledge God's creation of humankind as male and female and the unchangeable standard of Christian marriage between one man and one woman as the proper place for sexual intimacy and the basis of the family. We repent of our failures to maintain this standard and call for a renewed commitment to lifelong fidelity in marriage and abstinence for those who are not married.

We gladly accept the Great Commission of the risen Lord to make disciples of all nations, to seek those who do not know Christ and to baptise, teach and bring new believers to maturity.

We are mindful of our responsibility to be good stewards of God's creation, to uphold and advocate justice in society, and to seek relief and empowerment of the poor and needy.

We are committed to the unity of all those who know and love Christ and to building authentic ecumenical relationships. We recognise the orders and jurisdiction of those Anglicans who uphold orthodox faith and practice, and we encourage them to join us in this declaration.

We celebrate the God-given diversity among us which enriches our global fellowship, and we acknowledge freedom in secondary matters. We pledge to work together to seek the mind of Christ on issues that divide us.

We reject the authority of those churches and leaders who have denied the orthodox faith in word or deed. We pray for them and call on them to repent and return to the Lord.

We rejoice at the prospect of Jesus' coming again in glory, and while we await this final event of history, we praise him for the way he builds up his church through his Spirit by miraculously changing lives.

The Road Ahead

We believe the Holy Spirit has led us during this week in Jerusalem to begin a new work. There are many important decisions for the development of this fellowship which will take more time, prayer and deliberation.

Among other matters, we shall seek to expand participation in this fellowship beyond those who have come to Jerusalem, including cooperation with the Global South and the Council of Anglican Provinces in Africa. We can, however, discern certain milestones on the road ahead.

Primates' Council

We, the participants in the Global Anglican Future Conference, do hereby acknowledge the participating Primates of GAFCON who have called us together, and encourage them to form the initial Council of the GAFCON movement. We look forward to the enlargement of the Council and entreat the Primates to organize and expand the fellowship of confessing Anglicans.

We urge the Primates' Council to authenticate and recognise confessing Anglican jurisdictions, clergy and congregations and to encourage all Anglicans to promote the gospel and defend the faith.

We recognise the desirability of territorial jurisdiction for provinces and dioceses of the Anglican Communion, except in those areas where churches and leaders are denying the orthodox faith or are preventing its spread, and in a few areas for which overlapping jurisdictions are beneficial for historical or cultural reasons.

We thank God for the courageous actions of those Primates and provinces who have offered orthodox oversight to churches under false leadership, especially in North and South America. The actions of these Primates have been a positive response to pastoral necessities and mission opportunities. We believe that such actions will continue to be necessary and we support them in offering help around the world.

We believe this is a critical moment when the Primates' Council will need to put in place structures to lead and support the church. In particular, we believe the time is now ripe for the formation of a province in North America for the federation currently known as Common Cause Partnership to be recognised by the Primates' Council.

Conclusion: Message from Jerusalem

We, the participants in the Global Anglican Future Conference, were summoned by the Primates' leadership team to Jerusalem in June 2008 to deliberate on the crisis that has divided the Anglican Communion for the past decade and to seek direction for the future. We have visited holy sites, prayed together, listened to God's Word preached and expounded, learned from various speakers and teachers, and shared our thoughts and hopes with each other.

The meeting in Jerusalem this week was called in a sense of urgency that a false gospel has so paralysed the Anglican Communion that this crisis must be addressed. The chief threat of this dispute involves the compromising of the integrity of the church's worldwide mission. The primary reason we have come to Jerusalem and issued this declaration is to free our churches to give clear and certain witness to Jesus Christ.

It is our hope that this Statement on the Global Anglican Future will be received with comfort and joy by many Anglicans around the world who have been distressed about the direction of the Communion. We believe the Anglican Communion should and will be reformed around the biblical gospel and mandate to go into all the world and present Christ to the nations.

Jerusalem
Feast of St Peter and St Paul
29 June 2008

Latimer Publications

01 *The Evangelical Anglican Identity Problem* Jim Packer
02 *The ASB Rite A Communion: A Way Forward* Roger Beckwith
03 *The Doctrine of Justification in the Church of England* Robin Leaver
04 *Justification Today: The Roman Catholic and Anglican Debate* R. G. England
05/06 *Homosexuals in the Christian Fellowship* David Atkinson
07 *Nationhood: A Christian Perspective* O. R. Johnston
08 *Evangelical Anglican Identity: Problems and Prospects* Tom Wright
09 *Confessing the Faith in the Church of England Today* Roger Beckwith
10 *A Kind of Noah's Ark? The Anglican Commitment to Comprehensiveness* Jim Packer
11 *Sickness and Healing in the Church* Donald Allister
12 *Rome and Reformation Today: How Luther Speaks to the New Situation* James Atkinson
13 *Music as Preaching: Bach, Passions and Music in Worship* Robin Leaver
14 *Jesus Through Other Eyes: Christology in a Multi-Faith Context* Christopher Lamb
15 *Church and State Under God* James Atkinson
16 *Language and Liturgy* Gerald Bray, Steve Wilcockson, Robin Leaver
17 *Christianity and Judaism: New Understanding, New Relationship* James Atkinson
18 *Sacraments and Ministry in Ecumenical Perspective* Gerald Bray
19 *The Functions of a National Church* Max Warren
20/21 *The Thirty-Nine Articles: Their Place and Use Today* Jim Packer, Roger Beckwith
22 *How We Got Our Prayer Book* T. W. Drury, Roger Beckwith
23/24 *Creation or Evolution: a False Antithesis?* Mike Poole, Gordon Wenham
25 *Christianity and the Craft* Gerard Moate
26 *ARCIC II and Justification* Alister McGrath
27 *The Challenge of the Housechurches* Tony Higton, Gilbert Kirby
28 *Communion for Children? The Current Debate* A. A. Langdon
29/30 *Theological Politics* Nigel Biggar
31 *Eucharistic Consecration in the First Four Centuries and its Implications for Liturgical Reform* Nigel Scotland
32 *A Christian Theological Language* Gerald Bray
33 *Mission in Unity: The Bible and Missionary Structures* Duncan McMann
34 *Stewards of Creation: Environmentalism in the Light of Biblical Teaching* Lawrence Osborn
35/36 *Mission and Evangelism in Recent Thinking: 1974-1986* Robert Bashford
37 *Future Patterns of Episcopacy: Reflections in Retirement* Stuart Blanch
38 *Christian Character: Jeremy Taylor and Christian Ethics Today* David Scott
39 *Islam: Towards a Christian Assessment* Hugh Goddard
40 *Liberal Catholicism: Charles Gore and the Question of Authority* G. F. Grimes
41/42 *The Christian Message in a Multi-Faith Society* Colin Chapman
43 *The Way of Holiness 1: Principles* D. A. Ousley
44/45 *The Lambeth Articles* V. C. Miller
46 *The Way of Holiness 2: Issues* D. A. Ousley
47 *Building Multi-Racial Churches* John Root
48 *Episcopal Oversight: A Case for Reform* David Holloway
49 *Euthanasia: A Christian Evaluation* Henk Jochemsen
50/51 *The Rough Places Plain: AEA 1995*
52 *A Critique of Spirituality* John Pearce
53/54 *The Toronto Blessing* Martyn Percy
55 *The Theology of Rowan Williams* Garry Williams
56/57 *Reforming Forwards? The Process of Reception and the Consecration of Woman as Bishops* Peter Toon
58 *The Oath of Canonical Obedience* Gerald Bray
59 *The Parish System: The Same Yesterday, Today And For Ever?* Mark Burkill
60 *'I Absolve You': Private Confession and the Church of England* Andrew Atherstone

Latimer Publications

61	*The Water and the Wine: A Contribution to the Debate on Children and Holy Communion* Roger Beckwith, Andrew Daunton-Fear	LB05	*Christ's Gospel to the Nations: The Heart & Mind of Evangelicalism Past, Present & Future* Peter Jensen
62	*Must God Punish Sin?* Ben Cooper	LB06	*Passion for the Gospel: Hugh Latimer (1485-1555) Then and Now. A commemorative lecture to mark the 450th anniversary of his martyrdom in Oxford* A. McGrath
63	*Too Big For Words?: The Transcendence of God and Finite Human Speech* Mark D. Thompson		
64	*A Step Too Far: An Evangelical Critique of Christian Mysticism* Marian Raikes	LB07	*Truth and Unity in Christian Fellowship* M. Nazir-Ali
65	*The New Testament and Slavery: Approaches and Implications* Mark Meynell		
66	*The Tragedy of 1662: The Ejection and Persecution of the Puritans* Lee Gatiss		
67	*Heresy, Schism and Apostasy* Gerald Bray		
68	*Paul in 3D: Preaching Paul as Pastor, Story-teller and Sage* Ben Cooper		
69	*Christianity and the Tolerance of Liberalism: J. Gresham Machen and the Presbyterian Controversy of 1922-1937* Lee Gatiss		
70	*An Anglican Evangelical Identity Crisis: The Churchman-Anvil Affair of 1981-1984* Andrew Atherstone		
GGC	*God, Gays and the Church* Ed. Nolland, Sugden & Finch		
AEID	*Anglican Evangelical Identity: Yesterday and Today* J.I.Packer, N.T.Wright		
WTL	*The Way, the Truth and the Life: Theological Resources for a Pilgrimage to a Global Anglican Future* Theological Resource Team of GAFCON		
WTC	*The Way of the Cross: Biblical Resources for a Global Anglican Future*		
IB	*The Anglican Evangelical Doctrine of Infant Baptism* John Stott, J. Alec Motyer		
LB01	*The Church of England: What it is, and what it stands for* R. T. Beckwith		
LB02	*Praying with Understanding: Explanations of Words and Passages in the Book of Common Prayer (2nd Edition)* R. T. Beckwith		
LB03	*The Failure of the Church of England? The Church, the Nation & the Anglican Communion* A. Pollard		
LB04	*Towards a Heritage Renewed* H. R. M. Craig		

www.ingramcontent.com/pod-product-compliance
Lightning Source LLC
Chambersburg PA
CBHW060848050426
42453CB00008B/895